THE
BHAGAVAD
GITA

Translated from the Sanskrit by
JUAN MASCARÓ
With an introduction by
SIMON BRODBECK

PENGUIN BOOKS

PENGUIN BOOKS

Published by the Penguin Group
Penguin Books Ltd, 80 Strand, London WC2R ORL, England
Penguin Putnam Inc., 375 Hudson Street, New York, New York 10014, USA
Penguin Books Australia Ltd, 250 Camberwell Road, Camberwell, Victoria 3124, Australia
Penguin Books Canada Ltd, 10 Alcorn Avenue, Toronto, Ontario, Canada M4V 3B2
Penguin Books India (P) Ltd, 11 Community Centre, Panchsheel Park, New Delhi – 110 017, India
Penguin Books (NZ) Ltd, Cnr Rosedale and Airborne Roads, Albany, Auckland, New Zealand
Penguin Books (South Africa) (Pty) Ltd, 24 Sturdee Avenue, Rosebank 2196, South Africa

Penguin Books Ltd, Registered Offices: 80 Strand, London WC2R ORL, England

www.penguin.com

This translation first published 1962
Reprinted with new Chronology, Introduction and Further Reading 2003

5

Copyright © Juan Mascaró, 1962
Chronology, Introduction and Further Reading copyright © Simon Brodbeck, 2003
All rights reserved

Set in 10.5/13pt Monotype Bembo
By Datix International Limited, Bungay, Suffolk
Printed in England by Clays Ltd, St Ives plc

PENGUIN CLASSICS

THE BHAGAVAD GITA

ADVISORY EDITOR: BETTY RADICE

JUAN MASCARÓ was born in Majorca. The beauty of the island, then unspoilt, and the strength of the living folk tradition, made a deep impression on him as a child. At the age of thirteen he copied a book on occultism, but this proved spiritually misleading. However, he found a reading of the *Bhagavad Gita* highly illuminating, although it was a poor translation, and this led him to study the elements of Sanskrit. Later he went to Cambridge, where he read modern and oriental languages, Sanskrit, Pali and English.

He lectured in Oxford on the Spanish mystics, and then went to Ceylon, where he was Vice-Principal of Parameshvara College at Jaffna, and to the University of Barcelona, where he was Professor of English. After the Spanish Civil War he settled permanently in England. He lived at first on the hills above Tintern Abbey; he translated some *Upanishads* (also a Penguin Classic) and the *Bhagavad Gita*. He then returned to Cambridge University where he was a supervisor in English and lectured on 'Literary and Spiritual Values in the Authorized Version of the Bible'. He also translated the *Dhammapada* from Pali for the Penguin Classics. He married Miss Kathleen Ellis in 1951 and they had a son and a daughter. Juan Mascaró died in 1987. *The Times* obituary described him as a man who had 'achieved the unique feat of translation from languages not his own (Sanskrit and Pali) into another language not at first his own (English). His aim – decried by some academic critics but appreciated by thousands of readers all over the world – was to convey the essence of the original in pure, poetic English . . . His translations of the *Gita*, *Upanishads* and *Dhammapada* are the best that we have in English, and are unlikely to be superseded.'

SIMON PEARSE BRODBECK was born in 1970 in Lancaster and grew up in the Lune Valley. After attending the local comprehensive school, he studied at the universities of Cambridge and London, completing his PhD thesis, 'Action without attachment in the *Bhagavad Gita*', at the School of Oriental and African Studies. He is currently teaching part-time and pursuing further research on the *Mahabharata*. He is married and his interests include philosophy, gender studies, cricket and gardening.

CONTENTS

ACKNOWLEDGEMENTS

The translator wishes to tender grateful acknowledgements to the following for permission to quote copyright passages in his Introduction:

Methuen & Co., Publishers, Ltd, London, for quotations from the *Vedas*, translated by J. Mascaró in his Anthology *Lamps of Fire*.

John Murray, Publishers, Ltd, London, for quotations from the *Upanishads*, translated by J. Mascaró under the title *Himalayas of the Soul*.

J.M.

This volume is dedicated to Hugh l'Anson Fausset.

CHRONOLOGY

Dating Indian texts is extremely difficult, partly because many of them were continuously compiled over long periods. The vagueness of the following scheme reflects this.

3102 BCE	traditional dating of *Mahabharata* war (discredited)
2500–1600 BCE	peak of Indus (and Sarasvati) Valley civilization
1500–800 BCE	composition of the Vedic hymns
c. 800 BCE	rise of iron technology in India
800–200 BCE	composition of the major *Upanishads*
563–483 BCE	life of the Buddha
540–468 BCE	life of Mahavira, founder of Jainism
500 BCE–500 CE	compilation of the *Mahabharata*, including the *Bhagavad Gita*
1785	*Bhagavad Gita* first translated into English, by Charles Wilkins

INTRODUCTION

The *Bhagavad Gita* is a small excerpt of the *Mahabharata*. The *Mahabharata* is the larger of the two Indian epics, the other being the *Ramayana*. The period of their composition, 500 BCE–500 CE, was one of extreme textual proliferation. Both epics intriguingly present the kind of esoteric discourse (on various ritual, cosmological and religio-philosophical matters) prevalent amongst the Brahminical priestly-academic élite, within a framework derived from more popular storytelling traditions. Each is a story, a narrative of various characters and their adventures. Other stories are also told within the narrative, and the main characters reflect on these stories in ways which suggest how the reader might reflect on theirs. Although the Sanskrit epics were more or less fixed in their extended, digressional literary format in the early centuries of the Common Era, their stories exist in diverse versions in dramatic, bardic and literary contexts which continue to change and develop in the present day.

The *Bhagavad Gita* takes place at a critical point deep within the *Mahabharata*. Two vast armies stand mustered and almost ready to close in battle. The assembled warriors come from the length and breadth of the known world. The dispute they hope to resolve is one of kingdom and honour between rival sets of cousins, the Pandavas, sons of Pandu, and the Kauravas, sons of Dhritarashtra, Pandu's blind elder brother. Though ineligible for kingship, Dhritarashtra has been regent of the realm and guardian of the crown princes after Pandu's early retirement and death. He had partitioned the kingdom, but his sons had arranged a gambling match, won a thirteen-year loan of the Pandavas' half, and then refused to return it, precipitating war.

Arjuna, the most distinguished warrior in the Pandava army, surveys his adversaries and expresses to Krishna, his charioteer and great friend, his resolve not to fight. The opposing forces contain many with whom the Pandavas have no quarrel: moreover, these include highly esteemed teachers and elders. Arjuna's scruples centre on the imagined personal consequences of fighting: his guilt for the decimation of his people. Krishna speaks with him – the *Bhagavad Gita* is their dialogue – until he is once more resolved to fight. Subsequently the war is fought for eighteen days, leaving only a handful of warriors alive, and the Pandavas, though outnumbered at the start, emerge victorious due to devious and unchivalrous tactics suggested by Krishna.

Krishna's response to Arjuna's dejection is lengthy because Arjuna does not respond to the methods initially employed to motivate him. Elsewhere in the *Mahabharata*, before other battles, warriors pale at their prospects, but are ordinarily set fighting by charioteers mocking their cowardice, recalling the exploits of previous heroes, and talking up the consequences of victory as well as the noble death and heavenly afterlife of those who fall in battle. Arjuna is not open to persuasion on these terms, and accordingly Krishna holds forth on loftier topics. He outlines a holistic view of the world's functioning, and of the place of human action in general, and Arjuna's martial action in particular, in the grand scheme of things.

It seems that Arjuna is persuaded to fight because Krishna has inspired him to believe that there is an attitude that can be taken by a person towards his or her activities which maximizes the creative benefit of those activities as well as ensuring that psychological and spiritual ill-effects do not accrue to the individual concerned. Krishna calls this attitude *yoga*, and explains that it is a general attitude, applicable to all activities, not just war, and available to all people, not just Arjuna. This is why the *Bhagavad Gita* is commonly found extracted from its *Mahabharata* context and used by millions of Hindus and many others as a guide to a spiritual way of being and behaving. It is clear from the *Mahabharata* that the text's creators allowed the narrative to be suspended at this dramatic moment partly so that its audience would be encouraged to apply Krishna's attitude in their own activities. Indeed, although revolutionary on an internal level for the person applying it, this attitude is particularly conducive to social harmony and cultural continuity within a diverse, organized and potentially enormous community. The person successfully applying Krishna's yogic attitude is described as behaving traditionally, participating in existing institutions and helping to sustain the community. The process of individual salvation is private, and compatible with all walks of life even in their apparently more unpleasant moments.

Because Arjuna agrees to fight after hearing Krishna's speech, we suppose that he is convinced by the *Bhagavad Gita*'s exposition of the yogic attitude. However, it is not clear from the *Mahabharata* whether or not he managed to fight in the manner suggested. He does not seem as troubled in the wake of the battle as his eldest brother Yudhishthira, but we would expect this since it is Yudhishthira, the story's central character, who must rule in the new, changed world. But just as the yogic method is a private affair, so are its individual results. The epic, unlike the modern novel, does not enter the internal worlds of its characters. It describes them exclusively from without, and so is unable to comment on whether or not Arjuna receives the subtle existential, psychological and spiritual benefits which would follow from successful *yoga*. Later on in the *Mahabharata*, Arjuna tells Krishna that he has forgotten what was said just before the battle, and asks for a repeat performance, which

Krishna is scarcely able to provide. This could suggest that Arjuna has not become a *yogi*, or, equally, that he has already done so in part and now wishes to perfect his art.

Knowledge of Dehin, *the 'One in the Body'*

Krishna's presentation of the yogic method is built upon his revelation of certain truths concerning the composition of the universe as a whole and of the individuals within it. With respect to Arjuna's specific fears about killing, Krishna introduces the idea of *dehin*, the 'one in the body' ('spirit', 'soul'), which cannot be killed, and which will repeatedly take another body after the death of the current one. The essential aspect of a human being is thus radically recontextualized. The unit under consideration is no longer an individual, whose life is short and precarious and may be suddenly ended despite protective efforts. Instead, it is an extended sequence of individual lives. Each life in the sequence is connected directly to the immediately preceding and following lives, and indirectly to every other life in the same sequence. The *dehin* represents the unity of any particular sequence of lives. In each life, it witnesses whatever takes place physically within the range of the senses and sensations of a particular individual's body. It also witnesses the mental world of that individual, its thoughts and emotions.[1] The apparent self-consciousness of the individual is in fact the *dehin*'s consciousness of the individual. But the *dehin* only witnesses. It cannot make the individual act, think or feel in any one way rather than another. From its point of view, all actual events, thoughts and feelings take care of themselves, as it were. They follow their own laws: they are causally related to each other, but not to *dehin*. But it may be misleading to talk here of *dehin*'s 'point of view', since *dehin* has no point of view of its own: at any particular time it has the point of view of a particular individual. It is proposed as a hypothetical subject only in order to modify the simple, single-bodied subject identity of the individual. It witnesses what the individual feels and thinks to itself, but it cannot think anything about those thoughts to *it*self, or have any reaction or response. Reaction and response there are, but these are the business of the individual and its world of process, not of *dehin*. If the idea of *dehin* comes within the range of an individual, and is thought about by that individual, then, Krishna suggests, the response within that individual will be a reduction of attachment and trauma, and an ability to cope with all activities and eventualities, even those involving the death of its loved ones or of itself.

This *dehin*, also known in the *Bhagavad Gita* as *atman* ('self'), *purusha* (literally 'person') and *kshetrajña* ('knower of the field'), was widely theorized in ancient India. The Jains called it *jiva*. The Buddhists, though they did not theorize such an entity, accepted the idea of sequences of abutting lives, conceiving these as chains of links with no common core, rather than as strings of beads. The idea of salvation emerged in various milieux, centred on the possibility of *moksha* or *nirvana*, an end to a sequence of lives. Special mental and physical activities were pursued in order to help ensure, for a particular individual, either that this life be the last in the sequence, or, at the very least, that the last in this sequence might be imminent. Now, Arjuna is not involved in this pursuit of *moksha*. Until Krishna begins to hold forth, he has barely heard of the *dehin*. He is not trying to bring about the end of the sequence of lives he might be part of. His objection to fighting is not that it may hinder such an objective. Rather, he is worried about how he will live with himself for the rest of his current life, and fearful that his actions will produce an unpleasant afterlife for himself and his family. However, the pursuit of *moksha* was known to the text's audience, and thus the text expands the scope of the yogic method, which is said not only to remove the immediate psychological ill-effects of drastic actions, but also to remove the tendency of those actions to elongate a sequence of lives. This extension of the method's results beyond the scope demanded by Arjuna's situation was required because of the prevalence of the pursuit of *moksha* and its combination with the theory of *karma*. As theorized within renunciant groups and ideologies, another birth after death, that is, the prolonging of a sequence of lives, was only effected through outstanding *karma* or *karmabandha*, the 'bond of action', which was generated in particular by violent or passionate activity, such as that involved in war, ritual sacrifice, the production and protection of offspring, and the maintenance of social structures. The pursuit of *moksha* thus threatened social, cultural and economic continuity. The *Bhagavad Gita* attempts to remove this threat by proposing that actions, even apparently terribly destructive ones, will not result in the accumulation of any *karmabandha* at all if performed with a yogic, non-attached attitude (3.9, 9.28).

Knowledge of Prakriti, Material Nature

Krishna's yogic method is a powerful tool for personal transformation, since it is based on the truth that *dehin* is a quality or substance – neither word really fits – fundamentally set apart from *prakriti*, the natural world of physical, mental and emotional process, the coming to be and passing away of causally linked items, forces and phenomena. It is as if the idea of ending the sequences of lives in *moksha* or *nirvana* has been hypothesized to provide an opportunity for thinking about what the inactive, witnessing *dehin* could possibly be in and of itself, separate from anything it might witness. This is a daunting philosophical task, which the *Bhagavad Gita* does not attempt directly. Instead, the understanding of the truth of *dehin* is allied to the yogic method by the text's exploration of what *dehin* is not, that is, *prakriti*, the world of process, which may be studied and shown to account for its own permutations, as if it contains them all, even future ones, within itself. Conceiving of *prakriti* in this way is correlated with non-attachment and peace of mind in active individuals, for any actual activities an individual may undertake or be subject to are then known to be subsections of a causally sufficient network of forces extending immeasurably before and beyond that individual in time as well as in space.

As this is so for actual activities, it is so also for imagined activities, such as Arjuna fighting and dying in battle, or Arjuna playing no part while his brothers and allies fight without him. These imagined activities are to be seen as the actual mental activities of someone's imagination. *Prakriti* governs the private psychological and existential aspects of the individual, all the things it says only to itself, as exhaustively as it governs the physics of visible behaviours. Krishna reveals (18.59–60, 11.34) that Arjuna's participation in the war, and a Pandava victory after the destruction of almost all the mustered warriors, are events that simply will come to pass. They are already contained within the world. Arjuna cannot help but fight, just as, by implication, he could not help but think, briefly, that he would not fight.

It seems to us, reading the text, that Arjuna agrees to fight only because Krishna has performed the *Bhagavad Gita*, persuading him to do so. We identify Krishna's speech as the cause of Arjuna's fighting. We can then say to ourselves that if Krishna had not spoken, Arjuna would not have fought. According to the logic of the text, however, there are problems with this conventional approach. Krishna did perform the *Bhagavad Gita*, so any suggestion of him not doing so is imaginary. If, given the circumstances (which include Krishna's speech), Arjuna cannot help but fight, then likewise Krishna, given the circumstances (which include Arjuna's refusal to fight), cannot help but speak as he does. The text explains any action to be the only possible outcome, given the current disposition of the person concerned (which includes their perception of the situation). If we then ask what exactly it is about the person's disposition and perception that makes the outcome unavoidable, we can answer in many different ways. We can make a list of hypothetical causal factors. Just now, when we identified (Arjuna's perception of) Krishna's speech as the cause of Arjuna's fighting, the list was a short one, because that speech was seen to be reason enough on its own. The list will end when we think sufficient reasons have been given to account for the event. But this list depends on what kinds of things we view as explanatory, rather than on the actual causes of the event. Many events happen, after all, without anybody offering explanations for them. Causal antecedents may discharge their function without being obvious to anyone or observable by anyone. A distinction must be made between, on the one hand, the actual reasons why an event occurs, and, on the other hand, the reasons we might give to ourselves to explain that event to our satisfaction. In light of this distinction we can see that, in an important sense, all reasons identified by words or thought are partial, biased, and largely imaginary. They do not refer to the external world, only to our internal world. Identified antecedents do not properly represent the pure, rational flux within which any event is embedded, which fills all space and time. At most they indicate the activity of identifying antecedents, that is, the production of a narrative, a supposedly descriptive mental or verbal text.

The inability of descriptions properly to represent the world is pointed out in the *Bhagavad Gita* through Krishna's idea of *maya* (the 'cloud of appearance', 7.14–15), the natural predicament of individuals in matters of knowledge. We attempt to represent reality, reifying subsections of *prakriti*'s flux through an interplay of signs, but we find that we cannot be properly expressive, either to ourselves or to each other, because our conscious expressions can do no more than rearrange existing symbolic forms and dualisms. We are bound by existing linguistic conventions of description and explanation. Arjuna's verbal expression demonstrates this. He describes the war in conventional terms: it is obligatory, since warriors must preserve their honour, avenge treachery, and oppose tyrants; but it is also forbidden, since relatives and teachers may not be killed. So his participation in the war is simply inexplicable, and this is why he cannot countenance it. Krishna's point is that conventional explanations of Arjuna's fighting need play no part at all in Arjuna's actually fighting. Why should what happens be explicable? The very fact of it happening is explanation enough. Since there are conventions which urge that the battle must be fought, as well as equally strong ones which urge the opposite, these conventions themselves have been shown to be of no use. They demonstrably fail to represent reality, and so the conventional distinctions between correct and incorrect behaviour, and between true and false descriptions, will have to dissolve. This is why Krishna gives no direct answer to Arjuna's dilemma. He does not supply any ethical arguments to explain that, in this case, the reasons to fight outweigh the reasons not to. He bypasses conventional explanations. The actual reasons for Arjuna's fighting cannot be known. They do not exist in any language.

The Individual Ego

Krishna's proposal of action without attachment is specifically concerned with attachment to the consequences or fruits of action. Though actions do have consequences, these need not be represented or known. *Prakriti* automatically connects every event to others, but its workings are impenetrable to us. In particular, our knowledge of the past and the future is notoriously deficient, reduced to stories told in the present. Both the causes and the results of an activity are unavailable. Krishna makes it clear that focusing on imaginary results creates great suffering, and suggests that it be minimized. He stresses that present actions are fully taken care of. They are contained by the unique present state of the world. The future is taken care of, moment by moment, in the same way: it need not and will not correspond to anything imaginable, and the proliferation of imagined visions of it may severely affect the attitude with which actions are performed, causing suffering in the short term and rebirth in the long term.

Imaginary futures within an individual's mind tend to cluster around an idea of 'I'. The 'I' is supposed to serve as the recipient of the individual's past, present and future experience, and also as the agent of its conscious activities. However, as we have seen, the recipient of experience can only be *dehin*. In any case, the vast majority of physical and mental events, being sub-conscious, are no more experienced than is the rain by the earth, even though they clearly happen to the individual and have an effect upon it. Yet the individual's conscious activities are regulated by *prakriti* no less than its unconscious ones, and so, if an agent is to be isolated, it must be *prakriti*. The agent of action is thus as different as it possibly could be from the recipi-ent of experience, and the conflation of the two into an ego is a fundamental mistake. Krishna shows how natural such a mistake is for individuals, who are spatially discrete, independently mobile, sense-dependent, short-lived, preoccupied with their own survival and that of their offspring, and who furthermore refer to themselves and to each other in discourse using specific names and pronouns. But the individual is only unitary at a structural level from certain points of view and for certain pur-poses, and so 'I' is no more than a sign amongst others: it denotes no metaphysical entity. Nonetheless, in the context of a highly populated and genetically diverse society, institutions of accountability take this strange 'I' very seriously, making judgements not just on the basis of actions performed, but also on the basis of the story the acting individual may tell of its actions. From the *Bhagavad Gita*'s point of view, the story told by an acting individual about its actions, even the story told to itself alone, is irrelevant to those actions themselves: it does not govern them. The text suggests that actions be undertaken without intention ('fanciful thought', 4.19; 'earthly will', 6.2 and 4), that is, without any story being told to link an 'I' to a set of imaginary consequences. Such stories denote the operation of desire and aversion, the mental ingredients of attachment. The *yogi* is said to act without imagining the action's success or failure (however these might be construed), offering all actions, even mental ones, in an attitude of sacrifice or consecration. Now, this constraint on the *yogi*'s mentality towards actions performed, effectively places that mentality beyond the reach of our conventionally comprehensible descriptions, which are teleologically oriented by the conventional 'I'. Accordingly, all statements which purport to describe the *yogi*'s mentality of action directly – rather than obliquely, in terms of what it does *not* involve – must be taken in a more or less metaphorical sense.

The Bhagavad Gita*'s Authorial Agenda*

The *Bhagavad Gita*'s choice of metaphors can be shown to correlate with certain specific discourses prevalent in ancient India. The text demonstrates a high degree of intertextual awareness on the part of its creators, quoting, it seems, from Upanishadic sources,[2] and appropriating technical terms from many discursive ritual, cosmological and religio-philosophical traditions. To this extent, the text cannot be understood without an awareness of what its creators and transmitters may have sought to do by means of it: we must observe whose interests were served, and in what ways, by the text's production and nurture. It is clear that, around Kurukshetra where the battle is set, the Brahminical ritual economy, based on the authority of the Vedic tradition,[3] was in disrepair following the rise of renunciant, *moksha-* or *nirvana*-oriented groups and ideologies, principally those of the Buddhists, Jains and Ajivikas. Furthermore, the political function that the great rituals had discharged in earlier, more volatile times was not quite to the point in a cosmopolitan culture now connected through trade and through the Sanskrit language and its literature. The *Bhagavad Gita* paints a jaded picture of some of the rituals' more unsavoury contemporary adherents, 'who have no vision, and yet they speak many words. They follow the letter of the *Vedas*, and they say: "There is nothing but this." Their soul is warped with selfish desires, and their heaven is a selfish desire. They have prayers for pleasures and power, the reward of which is earthly rebirth. Those who love pleasure and power hear and follow their words . . .' (2.42–4: 'power' here is no more than local celebrity). But the text nonetheless seeks to safeguard the ritual economy. Despite having already suggested that the free will of the 'I' is meaningless, and that the 'correct thing' always happens, the text repeatedly insists that Arjuna – and, by implication, people in general – follow the established ritual texts as a guide to behaviour, and comply with the duties set down by male Brahmins as appropriate to his gender and social class, not least amongst which is paying male Brahmins for their services. Krishna explains in Chapter 3 that the institution of ritual sacrifice is required in order to safeguard the very regularity of nature upon which individuals depend for their existence. Thus the *yogi* is said to act 'for the good of all the world' (3.25). Now, if this is taken to mean that the *yogi* acts deliberately, motivated by desire for a certain universally beneficent state of affairs, then this would contradict what has already been said about the *yogi*, for 'the good of all the world' is then a likely candidate for egocentric attachment. Rather, this must be taken as an external description of what the *yogi* is doing; that is, it must be taken as a conventional recognition that his or her activities do, in practical reality, help to sustain the mechanisms and institutions of cosmic and social order. We are not told if or how the *yogi* consciously relates to those particular activities, beyond his or her knowing, generally, that all actual activities are absolutely necessary, and that no 'I' owns any of them.

The Personification of the Cosmic Process as Krishna

The *Bhagavad Gita* follows a tradition of analysing the human individual and the cosmos as a whole under the same structural pattern, drawing correspondences between the microcosm and the macrocosm. This tradition is common to the *Upanishads*. They equate *atman*, the individual's soul, with *brahman*, the cosmic soul. They also explain ritual activity in terms of the cosmic efficacy it embodies, identifying a structural equivalence between items of ritual apparatus and items of cosmic apparatus. Likewise the *Bhagavad Gita*, having identified *dehin* and *prakriti* as separable aspects and explanations of the individual, proceeds to apply the same structural analysis to the cosmos as a whole. Insofar as Arjuna represents the human archetype, Krishna represents the cosmic one. His *dehin* is the 'Spirit Supreme' (*purushottama*, literally 'highest person': see 8.1, 15.17–19) and his body is the totality of all *prakriti*. The prakritic individual comprises both the gross physical body and the subtle mental and emotional realm, and Krishna's *prakriti* is similarly subdivided. What to us is *dehin* is contained within Krishna's body as his higher *prakriti*. He calls it 'my invisible Spirit', 'the fountain of life' (7.5) and 'a spark of my eternal Spirit' (15.7). The destinies of our different *dehins*, each with its own particular sequence of lives, are, as it were, the inner mental events of the cosmic person. And just as the *dehin* leaves the body at the end of an individual's life, returning in another one only if there remains with it the residue of actions performed with attachment, so at the end of the cosmos, when the manifest play of *prakriti* ceases, the *purushottama* rests separate until the next 'day of Brahma', that is, the next cosmos (8.17–19, 9.7–10), which is brought about due to there remaining unmanifest *prakriti* (including, presumably, the karmic residues carried over by *dehins* from the previous cosmos).

The elegance of this analogy is considerable, and allows Krishna to speak both as the personification of the cosmos and as the personification of the *purushottama* which every cosmos depends on and has in common. However, if we question the analogy closely we can see a few rough edges. The individual body differs from the cosmic body in a very important way. As well as being connected to other bodies at its birth and death, the individual body is also spatially connected to a wider world, comprising inert and living bodies which it moves amongst and acts in response to. The cosmos, however, is always the only current item of its kind. This means that, though the agency of individuals may be dissolved into the wider prakritic environment, as suggested at 3.27 and 5.8–9, this option is not there for the personified cosmos, which must explain its actions – or have them explained by us – solely in terms of internal necessity. So when Arjuna is told that Krishna always acts with a yogic, non-attached attitude (3.22, 4.14), it is difficult to believe that this is the same yogic attitude recommended for Arjuna himself. It can only be the same attitude if these references are to Krishna the man, Arjuna's charioteer, not to the personified cosmos. Here, then, is the danger of a speaker using himself or herself as an analogue of the cosmos. One and the same pronoun – 'I' or 'me' – has to stand sometimes for the speaker, sometimes for the cosmos, sometimes for a particular element of the cosmos, be this manifest *prakriti* as a whole or the collection of *dehins* witnessing it, and sometimes for the extra-cosmic *purushottama*. It is not always clear which of these is being invoked. This problem occurs for us, as we read or hear the text, in a way that it would not have for Arjuna, since he knew Krishna far better than we do. Not only were they great human companions, but Arjuna also received the boon of 'divine sight' (11.8) and experienced Krishna's cosmic form directly, including, as it did, a preview of the future. Without having this experience ourselves, and without knowing the details of Arjuna's personal relationship with Krishna, it is difficult for us to know quite what to make of the frequent exhortations for Arjuna to exercise exclusive devotion or love (*bhakti*) for Krishna in all his thoughts and deeds.

Krishna-bhakti

The Krishna of popular legend and iconography is a blue-skinned, flute-playing boy-God. This Krishna, a subject of theology and widespread devotion, is not the Krishna of the *Mahabharata* but of other texts, most notably the *Harivamsha*, a late appendix to the *Mahabharata*, and the *Puranas*, particularly the *Vishnu Purana* (300–600 CE) and the *Bhagavata Purana* (800–1000 CE). The equation of these two Krishnas began whilst the *Mahabharata* was as yet unfinished. Though they form no part of its action, the earlier exploits of Krishna-as-a-boy are occasionally mentioned by some of its characters, thus grafting Krishna's epic activities on to a growing body of stories about a single divine figure, and enabling Krishna-*bhakti* in the *Bhagavad Gita* to be interpreted theologically within the Indian tradition. Within the European tradition, too, theological interpretations have been the norm. This is hardly surprising given that the *Bhagavad Gita* was approached by Europeans primarily as a religious text, and was understood by comparison with Judaeo-Christian theology, just as it had previously been understood by the Mughal emperors by comparison with Islamic theology. However, it may well be that theological interpretations are unnecessary, and that the scope of *bhakti* in the *Bhagavad Gita* can be fully exhausted by the text's narrative, cosmological and socio-political contexts.

In the narrative context, Krishna is the saviour of the Pandavas. It is only through his encouragement that they have the wherewithal to stage a concerted effort to reclaim their kingdom and redress the indignities that they have suffered. In danger at every stage of being distracted from their purpose by their family connection to their opponents, Arjuna and his brothers are deeply dependent on Krishna to maintain the focus of their resistance, and they loyally carry out his tactical suggestions even when deeply shocked by them. In fact, Krishna seems to have a political agenda of his own. His desire to see the Kauravas vanquished is based on anti-imperialistic principles which are evident in his dealings with other tyrants elsewhere in the *Mahabharata*. In an important sense the Pandavas are serving his interests rather than the other way round. Though to them the battle is a personal business, to him it is about long-term political stability across north India, which will affect them and their descendants in ways they do not necessarily appreciate. These considerations, which are not evident unless the *Bhagavad Gita* is considered within its *Mahabharata* context, can go a long way towards explaining why Krishna demands Arjuna's devotion through action.

In the cosmological context, Krishna-*bhakti* would allude to the *yogi*'s acting in full knowledge that all actions are as governed by Krishna's *prakriti* or Krishna-as-*prakriti*, and thus to the *yogi*'s offering, devoting or sacrificing those actions back to Krishna rather than appropriating them for a mistakenly postulated ego (5.8–10).

In the socio-political context of the text's early audiences, the idea of Krishna-*bhakti* facilitated and stabilized local power structures. Krishna is present in person within the world in many different forms as a protector of righteousness (4.6–8), and he is the recipient of all sacrifices and offerings no matter who these might ostensibly be intended for (9.23–4). When he lists 'some manifestations of my divine glory' (10.19–41), many of these are powers or personages held sacred by different communities in different milieux, which are now subsumed under an umbrella religion. The erection of such an umbrella may have eased inter-communal tensions, whilst allowing different rulers in different localities to maintain order and receive donations using the same symbol of authority and legitimacy. This technique is visible also within the *Puranas*. Though it gives the appearance of a theology, it may be understood in mundane terms.

The Bhagavad Gita *in its Indian and International Context*

Originally, the *Bhagavad Gita* was embedded within the context of the *Mahabharata*. However, as far as the use and interpretation of the *Bhagavad Gita* is concerned, it has usually functioned as a separate text. An enormous number of commentaries have been written on it. The status of the text within the Hindu tradition is such that thinkers have often sought to establish their spiritual authority by showing that their views can be derived from it. Accordingly, there is hardly a doctrine that it has not, at one time or another, been claimed to espouse. The earliest commentaries still extant are from the medieval period, most notably those of Shankara (788–820 CE) and Ramanuja (1017–1137), but the tradition of commentary is still very much alive. Only a small subsection of commentaries are public, however: millions of Hindus, and an increasing number of non-Hindus, use the *Bhagavad Gita* as a spiritual guide within their own lives, reading or hearing it regularly and bringing it to bear on their own situations by commenting on it to themselves.

The *Bhagavad Gita* was of particular use to Hindu intellectuals and public figures as Indian nationalist ideas began to emerge under British rule from the late eighteenth century onwards. The Hindu intellectual past was re-presented, to Hindus and colonials alike, in an attempt to show that Christian criticisms of Indian religion and culture were unfounded. In this context Hinduism was made to conform to Western ideas of what would constitute a religion, and the *Bhagavad Gita* was presented as its Bible. This resurgence of interest in the *Bhagavad Gita* in the Hindu tradition occurred at the same time as translations and discussions of the text began to appear in European circles. Whilst many such discussions were from an explicitly Christian perspective and were critical of what they perceived as the text's pantheistic and amoral outlook, many poets and philosophers in Europe and America were deeply inspired by it.

As the Indian nationalist movement grew, the *Bhagavad Gita* was interpreted in radically different ways by Hindu politicians. Bal Gangadhar Tilak (1856–1920), an extremist, wrote a commentary on it whilst imprisoned by the British. He stressed its rejection of quietism and its justification of violent action against tyrants, and used it to encourage revolutionary activity. Whilst Tilak's interpretation is very much in keeping with the *Mahabharata* context of the *Bhagavad Gita*, it does not tally with what we might expect of a so-called spiritual or religious text. Gandhi, on the other hand, read the text daily and saw the *Mahabharata* war as an allegorical representation of the internal struggle between the human soul and worldly temptations. For him, there was nothing in the text which contradicted his principles of non-violence and his politics of passive resistance. On the contrary, he saw his principles and politics as derived from the text.

Juan Mascaró's introduction to the text unites many of the interests which have moved interpreters ancient and modern, Indian and Western. He stands the *Bhagavad Gita* alongside the Greek and English literary classics, and introduces ideas derived from Christian morality ('sin' and 'forgiveness'), from European mysticism, and from post-Enlightenment rationalism (translating *buddhi* as 'reason'). He also uses the terminology of Vedanta (the Hindu school of philosophy based on the *Upanishads*), with its focus on *brahman* as *sat*, *cit* and *ananda* ('Being, Consciousness and Joy'), and shares Gandhi's view of the battle as allegorical. He expounds the text from many different angles with sustained and heartfelt passion. But he is misled when he suggests that it is pre-Buddhistic. Sections of it may be, and 'Buddhism' is a very vague term, but the *Bhagavad Gita* certainly responds to the anti-Vedic, anti-Brahminical discourse that Buddhism was part of.

Scholars increasingly view the *Bhagavad Gita* as narrowly as possible within its ancient historical and narrative context. At the same time, it continues to be used as a spiritual guide by readers from all walks of life. Moreover, it may be that the text has still more of a role to play in the future. Its deterministic natural philosophy has yet to be fully acknowledged, and may provide a liberating counterpoint to the ideological burden of freedom, choice and responsibility. What Arjuna and Krishna, if they ever existed, might have thought about this state of affairs, is anybody's guess. We can be sure, however, that if the creators of the *Mahabharata* had known the future of their text, they would have been delighted.

SIMON BRODBECK
February 2002

NOTES

1. I have used the impersonal pronoun 'it' to denote the individual because the individual is not necessarily a person. Though the individuals that the *Bhagavad Gita* concerns itself with are human ones, Indian traditions view even the lowliest of creatures as enlivened by *dehin*.

2. The *Upanishads* are a genre of speculative texts: see Translator's Introduction, below. There are particular similarities between sections of the *Bhagavad Gita* and sections of the *Katha* and *Shvetashvatara Upanishads*. These may be direct borrowings in one direction or the other, or common borrowings from other, lost texts.

3. The *Vedas* are predominantly concerned with rituals, containing hymns for use during them, instructions for their performance, and explanations of their necessity and meaning. See Translator's Introduction, below.

FURTHER READING

Unfortunately it has been nearly a hundred years since any translation of the whole *Mahabharata* was completed. Van Buitenen, the most recent scholar to attempt this mammoth task, managed only the first five of its eighteen books. Nonetheless, his translation is racy, excellently annotated and introduced, and extends almost up to the beginning of the war (J. A. B. van Buitenen, editor and translator, *The Mahabharata*, 3 vols., Chicago University Press, 1973–8). For a study of some of the *Mahabharata*'s most important issues, see Peter Hill, *Fate, Predestination and Human Action in the Mahabharata: A study in the history of ideas* (Munshiram Manoharlal, New Delhi, 2001). For a study placing Krishna's philosophy firmly in its *Mahabharata* context, see S. S. More, *Krishna, the Man and His Mission: An enquiry into the rationale of inter-relationship between Krishna's life, mission and philosophy* (Gaaj Prakashan, Poona, 1995).

There are a number of good introductory books about Hinduism, most notably J. L. Brockington, *The Sacred Thread: Hinduism in its continuity and diversity* (Edinburgh University Press, 1981; second edition 1996); Gavin Flood, *An Introduction to Hinduism* (Cambridge University Press, 1996); and Julius Lipner, *Hindus: Their religious beliefs and practices* (Routledge, London, 1994; paperback edition 1998). Amongst Indian texts, the *Upanishads* have the greatest overlap with the concerns of the *Bhagavad Gita*: see Valerie J. Roebuck, editor and translator, *The Upanishads* (Penguin, New Delhi, 2000).

For in-depth studies of particular recent commentators, see Robert N. Minor, ed., *Modern Indian Interpretations of the Bhagavad Gita* (State University of New York Press, Albany, 1986). Another useful collection of recent views is Julius Lipner, ed., *The Fruits of Our Desiring: An enquiry into the ethics of the Bhagavad Gita for our times* (Bayeux Arts, Calgary, 1997).

There is a good deal of crossover between the *Bhagavad Gita* and modern philosophy. The free will / determinism debate usually operates in terms far removed from those of the *Bhagavad Gita*: a welcome exception, which includes a sympathetic account of the determinist's attitude to action, is T. Honderich, *How Free Are You? The determinism problem* (Oxford University Press, 1993). Regarding the scientific implications of the *Bhagavad Gita*'s agnostic but faithful view of natural law, the interpretation of statistical methodology in quantum mechanics is highly instructive: see Christopher Norris, *Quantum Theory and the Flight from Realism: Philosophical responses to quantum mechanics* (Routledge, London, 2000). It is to be noted that the two authors named in this paragraph, whose views are – unknowingly – in line with those of the *Bhagavad Gita*, are firmly opposed by the majority of their peers.

Also recommended is Cormac McCarthy, *Blood Meridian, or The evening redness in the west* (Picador, London, 1990). This novel has resonances with the *Bhagavad Gita* on many levels. It is set in a time of violence, uncertainty and rapid change, against which is expounded a philosophy of detachment in action.

TRANSLATOR'S INTRODUCTION TO 1962 EDITION

The first translation from Sanskrit into English was a translation of the *Bhagavad Gita*. It was done by Charles Wilkins in 1785. Later on, when Alexander Hamilton, 1765–1824, was returning from India in 1802 and was obliged to stay in Paris because of the war, he taught Sanskrit to Friedrich von Schlegel, 1772–1829, the great German critic, who with romantic enthusiasm spread the knowledge of Sanskrit in Germany; and Schlegel's brother August translated the *Bhagavad Gita* into Latin.

The study of Sanskrit led to the comparative study of languages. It was found that Sanskrit, Persian, Greek and Latin, and also the Celtic, Germanic and Slavonic languages come from a primitive unwritten language called Aryan. From Ireland to India, and all over Europe and America, Aryan languages are spoken.

For over 3,000 years there has been an uninterrupted Sanskrit culture in India, if we include the Sanskrit of the *Vedas*, and Panini produced about 300 BC a perfect Sanskrit grammar, 'the shortest and fullest grammar in the world'.

Sanskrit literature is a great literature. We have the great songs of the *Vedas*, the splendour of the *Upanishads*, the glory of the *Bhagavad Gita*, the vastness of the *Mahabharata*, the tenderness and heroism found in the *Ramayana*, the wisdom of the fables and stories of India, the scientific philosophy of the Sankhya, the psychological philosophy of Yoga, the poetical philosophy of Vedanta, the laws of Manu, the grammar of Panini and other scientific writings, the lyrical poetry and drama culminating in the great poetry and dramas of Kalidasa.

There are, however, two great branches of literature not found in Sanskrit. There is no history and there is no tragedy: there is no Herodotus or Thucydides; and there is no Aeschylus or Sophocles or Euripides.

Sanskrit literature is, on the whole, a romantic literature interwoven with idealism and practical wisdom, and with a passionate longing for spiritual vision. There is a prayer in the *Vedas* which for over 3,000 years has been every morning on the lips of millions of Indians. It is the famous GAYATRI:

> TAT SAVITUR VARENIAM
>
> BHARGO DEVASYA DHIMAHI
>
> DHIYO YO NAH PRACHODAYAT

'Let our meditation be on the glorious light of Savitri. May this light illumine our minds.' The poet of the *Vedas* who chanted these words saw into the future: the mind of India has never tired in the search for Light.

Greece and India give us complementary views of the world. In the Greek temple we find the clear perfection of beauty: in the Indian temple we find the sublime sense of Infinity. Greece gives us the joy of eternal beauty in the outer world; and India gives us the joy of the Infinite in the inner world.

In these verses of Keats on a Grecian urn we find Greece:

> O Attic shape! fair attitude! with breed
> Of marble men and maidens overwrought,
> With forest branches and the trodden weed;
> Thou, silent form, dost tease us out of thought
> As doth eternity. Cold Pastoral!
> When old age shall this generation waste,

> Thou shalt remain, in midst of other woe
> Than ours, a friend to man, to whom thou say'st
> 'Beauty is truth, truth beauty, – that is all
> Ye know on earth, and all ye need to know.'

And Wordsworth in 'Tintern Abbey' gives us the spirit of India:

> And I have felt
> A presence that disturbs me with the joy
> Of elevated thoughts; a sense sublime
> Of something far more deeply interfused,
> Whose dwelling is the light of setting suns,
> And the round ocean and the living air,
> And the blue sky, and in the mind of man:
> A motion and a spirit, that impels
> All thinking things, all objects of all thought,
> And rolls through all things.

In the *Vedas*, composed long before writing was introduced into India, and before grammarians could analyse language, we see man watching the outside world with joy and wonder. He feels life and he prays for victory in life. He watches the beauty of the dawn and the glory of the sun and he feels that fire and air, and the waters and the winds are living powers: he offers to them the fire of sacrifice. His life depends upon nature, and he knows that between nature and himself there is not an impassable gulf. Man loves this beautiful creation and he feels that his love cannot but be answered by a greater Love. And he sings to Varuna, the God who loves and forgives:

These words of glory to the God who is light shall be words supreme amongst things that are great. I glorify Varuna almighty, the God who is loving towards him who adores.

We praise thee with our thoughts, O God. We praise thee even as the sun praises thee in the morning: may we find joy in being thy servants.

Keep us under thy protection. Forgive our sins and give us thy love.

God made the rivers to flow. They feel no weariness, they cease not from flowing. They fly swiftly like birds in the air.

May the stream of my life flow into the river of righteousness. Loose the bonds of sin that bind me. Let not the thread of my song be cut while I sing; and let not my work end before its fulfilment.

Remove all fear from me, O Lord. Receive me graciously unto thee, O King. Cut off the bonds of afflictions that bind me: I cannot even open mine eyes without thy help.

Let the dread weapons that wound the sinner hurt us not. Let us not go from light into darkness.

We will sing thy praises, O God almighty. We will now and evermore sing thy praises, even as they were sung of old. For thy laws are immutable, O God: they are firm like the mountains.

Forgive the trespasses that I may have committed. Many mornings remain to dawn upon us: lead us through them all, O God.

Rig Veda 11.28. 1–9

Sometimes the seer of the *Vedas* has the consciousness of transgression of a spiritual law: there has been a sin of ignorance or weakness, or even a sin of ill-will. In repentance he asks for forgiveness and has faith that love forgives sins:

He placed apart the heaven and the earth. He set in motion the sun and the stars and spread our earth before them. His greatness gave wisdom to the children of men.

And I speak with mine own heart and I ask: How shall I have communion with my God? What offerings of mine will he accept without anger? When shall I with a glad heart find his mercy?

I ask others for I would fain know my sin: I seek the wise and I ask them And one answer the sages give me: God, Varuna, is angry with thee.

What hath been, O my God, my transgression? Why wouldst thou slay thy friend who sings praises to thee? Tell me, all-powerful God, that pure from sin may I hasten to thee in adoration.

Loose from us the sins of our fathers. Forgive us our own sins, O Lord.

It was not my will, it was an illusion. It was thoughtlessness or anger or wine. The stronger is near to lead astray the weaker: even sleep can lead men to sin.

May I serve my God, the all-merciful. May I serve my jealous God free from sin. Our God gives wisdom to the simple; and leadeth the wise unto the path of good.

May this song of praise come to thee, O Varuna: may this song of praise abide in thine heart. May it be well with our rest and our labour. May thy blessings be with us for evermore.

Rig Veda VII.86

In the *Vedas* we have the dawn of spiritual vision and also the dawn of human thought. In their sublime 'Song of Creation' they consider the beginning of things:

There was not then what is nor what is not. There was no sky, and no heaven beyond the sky. What power was there? Where? Who was that power? Was there an abyss of fathomless waters?

There was neither death nor immortality then. No signs were there of night or day. The ONE was breathing by its own power, in deep peace. Only the ONE was: there was nothing beyond.

Darkness was hidden in darkness. The all was fluid and formless. Therein, in the void, by the fire of fervour arose the ONE.

And in the ONE arose love. Love the first seed of soul. The truth of this the sages found in their hearts: seeking in their hearts with wisdom, the sages found that bond of union between being and non-being.

Who knows in truth? Who can tell us whence and how arose this universe? The gods are later than its beginning: who knows therefore whence comes this creation?

Only that god who sees in highest heaven: he only knows whence comes this universe, and whether it was made or uncreated. He only knows, or perhaps he knows not.

Rig Veda x.129

In the last verse of this poem we have the beginning of philosophical inquiry: the poet of the *Vedas* saw that for the progress of the mind man requires doubt and faith.

In the *Vedas* we have the dawn of spiritual insight. In the *Upanishads* we have the full splendour of an inner vision.

About 112 *Upanishads* have been printed in Sanskrit, but the most important ones are about eighteen. The two longest, the *Brihad-Aranyaka* and the *Chandogya*, cover about 100 pages each. The length of most of the others ranges from about three to thirty pages, and a few are longer. The *Isha Upanishad*, one of the most important, has only eighteen verses. The earliest parts of the *Upanishads* are in prose and they may date from about 700 BC. The verse *Upanishads* are generally much later. We know practically nothing of their authors: they seem to come from the Unknown.

From nature outside in the *Vedas*, man goes in the *Upanishads* into his own inner nature; and from the many he goes to the ONE. We find in the *Upanishads* the great questions of man, and their answer is summed up in two words: BRAHMAN and ATMAN. They are two names for one Truth, and the two are One and the same. The Truth of the Universe is BRAHMAN: our own inner Truth is ATMAN. The sacred OM is a name for both Brahman and Atman. This can be divided into three sounds, but the three roll into one: AUM. One of the meanings of OM is YES. Brahman, Atman, OM, is the positive Truth, the Yes, of all.

Around this central idea we have all the questions and answers, the stories, the great thoughts and, above all, the wonderful poetry of the *Upanishads*.

At the beginning of the *Kena Upanishad* we have these questions and answers:

Who sends the mind to wander afar? Who first drives life to start on its journey? Who impels us to utter these words?

What cannot be spoken with words, but that whereby words are spoken. Know that alone to be Brahman, the Spirit; and not what people here adore.

What cannot be thought with the mind, but that whereby the mind can think. Know that alone to be Brahman, the Spirit; and not what people here adore.

In the *Katha Upanishad* this question is asked by the boy Nachiketas when he meets the Spirit of Death:

'When a man dies, this doubt arises: some say "he is" and some say "he is not". Teach me the truth.'

The answer is the same as that of the *Bhagavad Gita*: 'The Atman, the Self, is never born and never dies.'

The spiritual experience of Atman is expressed in these words of the *Chandogya Upanishad*:

There is a Spirit which is mind and life, light and truth and vast spaces. He contains all works and desires and all perfumes and all tastes. He enfolds the whole universe, and in silence is loving to all.

This is the Spirit that is in my heart, smaller than a grain of rice, or a grain of barley, or a grain of mustard-seed, or a grain of canary-seed, or the kernel of a grain of canary-seed. This is the Spirit that is in my heart, greater than the earth, greater than the sky, greater than heaven itself, greater than all these worlds. This is the Spirit that is in my heart, this is Brahman.

If we ask where is Brahman, the Spirit of the Universe, the answer is given in the *Kena Upanishad*:

He is seen in nature in the wonder of a flash of lightning. He comes to the soul in the wonder of a flash of vision.

If the thinking mind is not satisfied with answers in words of beauty, the *Upanishads* have something more definite to say. If we ask definitely 'What is Brahman?' the answer in modern terms would be: 'Brahman cannot be defined because it is Infinite. It is beyond thought and beyond imagination. It is nothing in the mind and nothing outside the mind, nothing past or present or future. These are only conceptions in time and space. But the nearest conception of Brahman we can have is to say that it is a state of consciousness beyond time when SAT, CIT, and, ANANDA, Being and Consciousness and Joy are ONE.' We thus have the *Mandukya Upanishad* that explains the paradox that Brahman is all, and Brahman is nothing or no-thing:

OM. The eternal Word is all: what was, what is, and what shall be, and what beyond is in eternity. All is OM.

Brahman is all and Atman is Brahman. Atman, the Self, has four conditions.

The first condition is the waking life of outward-moving consciousness, enjoying the seven outer gross elements.

The second condition is the dreaming life of inner-moving consciousness, enjoying the seven subtle inner elements in its own light and solitude.

The third condition is the sleeping life of silent consciousness when a person has no desires and beholds no dreams.

The fourth condition is Atman in His own pure state: the awakened life of supreme consciousness. It is neither outer nor inner consciousness, neither semi-consciousness nor sleeping consciousness, neither mere consciousness nor unconsciousness. He is Atman, the Spirit Himself, that cannot be seen or touched, that is above all distinctions, beyond thought and ineffable. In the union with Him is the supreme proof of His reality. He is peace and love.

This short Upanishad goes on to say that Atman is OM. 'Its three sounds, A, U, and M, are the first three stages of consciousness. The word OM as one sound is the fourth state of supreme consciousness.' The *Kena Upanishad* says that 'He is known in the ecstasy of an awakening.'

As Atman, the Self in each one of us and in all, is Brahman, God, the Highest in us and in all, we might say that the problem of the moral law in the *Upanishads* is solved by fulfilling the words of Shakespeare in *Hamlet*. For 'self', however, we should understand, 'Self':

> This above all, – to thine own self be true;
> And it must follow, as the night the day,
> Thou canst not then be false to any man.

At the same time, if we consider that the essence of our Being, our Self, is joy, ANANDA, we might think of the words of Spinoza about virtue: 'Blessedness is not the reward of virtue: it is virtue itself. We do not find joy in virtue because we control our lusts: but, contrariwise, because we find joy in virtue we are able to control our lusts.'

The essence of the *Upanishads* is summed up in the words 'TAT TVAM ASI', 'That thou art'. Salvation is communion with Truth: 'SATYAM EVA JAYATE', says the *Mundaka Upanishad*, 'Truth is victory', to find truth is to conquer. The joy of the infinite is ever with us, but we do not know this truth. We are like the beggar in the story who had been begging all his life in the same place. He wanted to be rich, but he was poor. When he died they found a treasure of gold buried just under the place where he had been begging. If he had only known how easy it was to be rich! True knowledge of the Self does not lead to salvation: it is salvation. But this is not an intellectual knowledge or even a poetical vision: 'In the union with Him is the supreme proof of His reality.' We may read in the *Upanishads* that beyond our becoming there is our Being, that beyond suffering and sorrow there is Joy, that beyond the three stages of ordinary consciousness there is a fourth state of supreme Consciousness; but what we read are only words. We cannot know the taste of a fruit or of a wine by reading words about them: we must eat the fruit and drink the wine. The seers of the *Upanishads* did not establish a Church, or found a definite religion, but the seers of the Spirit in all religions agree that communion with the Highest is not a problem of words but of life.

It will be seen that the lofty doctrines of the *Upanishads* are doctrines for the few: the Himalayas of the Soul are not for all. Men want a simple concrete God, or even a graven image of a god. They want a rule of life, and above all they want love. The later seers of the *Upanishads* saw this and in the *Isha Upanishad* we have ideas that we also find in the *Bhagavad Gita*. Because of its importance it should be quoted in full:

Behold the Universe in the glory of God: and all that lives and moves on earth. Leaving the transient, find joy in the Eternal: set not your heart on another's possession.

Working thus, a man may wish for a life of a hundred years. Only actions done in God bind not the soul of man.

There are demon-haunted worlds, regions of utter darkness. Whoever in life rejects the Spirit goes to that darkness after death.

The Spirit, without moving, is swifter than the mind; the senses cannot reach Him: He is ever beyond them. Standing still, He overtakes those who run. To the ocean of His being the spirit of life leads the streams of action.

He moves, and He moves not. He is far, and He is near. He is within all, and He is outside all.

Who sees all beings in his own Self, and his own Self in all beings, loses all fear.

When a sage sees this great Unity and his Self has become all beings, what delusion and what sorrow can ever be near him?

The Spirit filled all with His radiance. He is incorporeal and invulnerable, pure and untouched by evil. He is the supreme seer and thinker, immanent and transcendent. He placed all things in the path of Eternity.

Into deep darkness fall those who follow action. Into deeper darkness fall those who follow knowledge.

One is the outcome of knowledge, and another is the outcome of action. Thus have we heard from the ancient sages who explained this truth to us.

He who knows both knowledge and action, with action overcomes death and with knowledge reaches immortality.

Into deep darkness fall those who follow the immanent. Into deeper darkness fall those who follow the transcendent.

One is the outcome of the transcendent, and another is the outcome of the immanent. Thus have we heard from the ancient sages who explained this truth to us.

He who knows both the transcendent and the immanent, with the immanent overcomes death and with the transcendent reaches immortality.

The face of truth remains hidden behind a circle of gold. Unveil it, O god of light, that I who love the true may see!

O life-giving sun, offspring of the Lord of creation, solitary seer of heaven! Spread thy light and withdraw thy blinding splendour that I may behold thy radiant form: that Spirit far away within thee is my own inmost Spirit.

May life go to immortal life, and the body go to ashes. OM. O my soul, remember past strivings, remember! O my soul, remember past strivings, remember!

By the path of good lead us to final bliss, O fire divine, thou god who knowest all ways. Deliver us from wandering evil. Prayers and adoration we offer unto thee.

The times of the *Vedas* were times of action, and of all human actions the sacrifice to the gods was the most important. This was a material sacrifice like the offerings to God in the Old Testament; but there is a tendency in man to go from the world of matter to the world of mind. Micah, the Hebrew prophet, about 720 BC, was not satisfied with the external sacrifice. He wanted an inner offering, and he says:

Wherewith shall I come before the Lord, and bow myself before the high God? Shall I come before him with burnt offerings, with calves of a year old?

Will the Lord be pleased with thousands of rams, or with ten thousands of rivers of oil? Shall I give my first-born for my transgression, the fruit of my body for the sin of my soul?

He hath shewed thee, O man, what is good; and what doth the

Lord require of thee, but to do justly, and to love mercy, and to walk humbly with thy God?

Micah did not give us the metaphysics of an inner sacrifice as the *Upanishads* do. They give us our inner I AM who is ours and not ours, because it is the I AM of all, the I AM of the universe. According to Coleridge, the higher Imagination is 'the repetition in the finite mind of the eternal act of creation in the infinite I AM'. This idea might lead to the *Upanishads*: the Infinite is ever in us and the finite in us can have communion with the Infinite.

If we consider the great words of the *Upanishads* TAT TVAM ASI, 'That thou art', we find that from the world outside we are going into our inner world; but the words can be interpreted in different ways. 'I am Brahman' or 'I am Atman' or 'I am God' may sound strange unless we take it in the true meaning that only the I AM in me is: my little personality is practically nothing. On the other hand, TAT TVAM ASI can be interpreted in the sense that only God is, or 'Only Thou art'. In both cases our little personality disappears, as indeed it does disappear in the fourth state of consciousness described in the *Mundaka Upanishad*. But if we wanted to retain our personality and adore a personal God, then we can imagine Him as a Master and imagine ourselves as servants. Ramakrishna, 1836–86, the Indian saint, describes it in these words:

There are three different paths to reach the Highest: the path of I, the path of Thou, and the path of Thou and I.

According to the first, all that is, was, or ever shall be is I, my higher Self. In other words, I am, I was, and I shall be for ever in Eternity.

According to the second, Thou art, O Lord, and all is Thine.

And according to the third, Thou art the Lord, and I am Thy servant, or Thy son.

In the perfection of any of these three ways, a man will find God.

Anonymous translation

The first way is the way of the *Upanishads* and of the *Vedanta*; the second way is the way of love, of Mary in the Gospels; the third way is the way of service, of Martha. The three ways have in common that what is important is something above our little self, whether we call this I AM, or 'Thou art', or whether we say, 'Thou art my Master.' In the three ways there is an absolute forgetfulness of our lower personality, and a recognition of a higher Personality. The Brahman of the *Upanishads* is, however, beyond all conception: it includes all, but it is beyond all. To become one with Brahman means a process of deep thought, before we can transcend thought. Love and work are easier ways.

The *Vedas* laid stress on the outer world, the world of action of the Immanent; and the *Upanishads* laid stress on the inner world, the world of knowledge of the Transcendent Spirit. In the *Isha Upanishad* we find the word Isha, God, and not the word Brahman, although the spirit of Brahman breathes through the *Upanishad*. We also find a harmony of action and knowledge, of the immanent and the transcendent. All action, including religious ritual, can be a means of reaching the inner meaning of things.

This vision of action with a consciousness of its meaning is interwoven in the *Bhagavad Gita* with the idea of love. If life or action is the finite and consciousness or knowledge is the Infinite, love is the means of turning life into Light, the bond of union between the finite and the Infinite. In all true love there is the love of the Infinite in the person or thing we love.

The *Bhagavad Gita* was included in the *Mahabharata*. This vast epic of over one hundred thousand shlokas, or couplets, is the longest poem in the world: about thirty times as long as *Paradise Lost*, and about 140 times as long as the *Bhagavad Gita*! About four-fifths of the poem are stories, and these are centred around the main story which is the story of a war.

The word Mahabharata, meaning the great Bharata, reminds us of Bharata, the son of Shakuntala, the founder of a dynasty of Indian kings. The story is told in the *Mahabharata*, and was used by Kalidasa in his great drama *Shakuntala*, the masterpiece of Indian poetry.

The main story of the *Mahabharata* centres around forces of good and evil represented, on the whole, as the Pandavas and the Kuravas. The father of Dhrita-rashtra and Pandu was the king of Hastinapura about fifty miles north-east of modern Delhi. At his death Pandu succeeded to the throne, as his eldest brother, Dhrita-rashtra, was blind. The sons of Pandu were Yudhishthira, Bhima, Arjuna, Nakula, and Sahadeva. We find their names in the first chapter of the *Bhagavad Gita*. Dhrita-rashtra had one hundred sons and the eldest was Duryodhana, the incarnation of evil. Pandu died and the blind king Dhrita-rashtra brought up in his palace the five sons of his brother. The Pandavas became great warriors and Dhrita-rashtra appointed the eldest, Yudhishthira, as heir-apparent. This was the cause of the great rivalry and in the end of the great war.

The *Mahabharata* has eighteen books and the great battle where Duryodhana and all his armies were destroyed lasted eighteen days. The *Bhagavad Gita* has eighteen chapters. There is no doubt that the war described in the *Mahabharata* is not symbolic and that it may even be based on historical fact; but the problem is different when we find the dialogue between Krishna and Arjuna set in a background of war. The *Mahabharata* is the growth of centuries and to include a story in the *Mahabharata* was a way of securing its immortality. We find in the vast poem the story later on developed in the *Ramayana*, the stories of Nala and Damayanti, Savitri, Shakuntala and king Dushyanta, and many others. The *Bhagavad Gita* is like a little shrine in a vast temple, a temple that is both a theatre and a fair of this world; and whilst the war in the *Mahabharata* may be meant as a real war it is obvious that the war in the

Bhagavad Gita has a symbolic meaning. The Arjuna and Krishna that we find in the rest of the *Mahabharata* are different beings from the Krishna and Arjuna of the *Bhagavad Gita*. We find in the *Gita* that there is going to be a great battle for the rule of a Kingdom; and how can we doubt that this is the Kingdom of Heaven, the kingdom of the soul? Are we going to allow the forces of light in us or the forces of darkness to win? And yet, how easy not to fight, and to find reasons to withdraw from the battle! In the *Bhagavad Gita* Arjuna becomes the soul of man and Krishna the charioteer of the soul.

When we think of the chariot of Arjuna we can remember the image of a chariot in the *Upanishads*, in Plato, in Buddha, in Blake, in Keats. Of these the most interesting for spiritual purposes is the chariot in Buddhism which is called 'He that runs in silence'; the wheels of the chariot are 'Right effort'; the driver is DHAMMA, or truth. The chariot leads to Nirvana, the Kingdom of Heaven. The end of the journey is 'The land which is free from fear'.

The use of external images for spiritual purposes is quite common. The Song of Songs was incorporated in the Bible and a spiritual meaning given to it. St John of the Cross uses the imagery of marriage to describe the supreme communion of love. In the Sanskrit book of stories, the *Hitopadesha*, we find the following interpretation of Hindu ritual:

> The Spirit in thee is a river. Its sacred bathing place is contemplation; its waters are truth; its banks are holiness; its waves are love. Go to that river for purification: thy soul cannot be made pure by mere water.

Here we have the spiritual interpretation of the material bathing in the Ganges. We can also remember how parables have always been used for spiritual symbols. When Jesus spoke his parables he never meant them as 'true stories' but as stories of Truth, symbols leading to Truth.

If we want to understand the spiritual meaning of the *Bhagavad Gita*, we had better forget everything concerning the great battle of the *Mahabharata* or the story of Krishna and Arjuna in the vast epic. A spiritual reader of the *Gita* will find in it the great spiritual struggle of a human soul. The war imagery is even used by Krishna in the poem when at the end of Chapter 3 he says: 'Be a warrior and kill desire, the powerful enemy of the soul'; and again at the end of Chapter 4: 'Kill therefore with the sword of wisdom the doubt born of ignorance that lies in thy heart.' How could the treachery, robbery, and butchery of war be reconciled with the spiritual vision and love of the *Bhagavad Gita*? How could we reconcile it with the Spirit of the *Gita*, and of all true spiritual seers, as expressed in those words of Krishna? 'And when a man sees that the God in himself is the same God in all that is, he hurts not himself by hurting others: then he goes indeed to the highest Path' 13.28.

Scholars differ as to the date of the *Bhagavad Gita*; but as the roots of this great poem are in Eternity the date of its revelation in time is of little spiritual importance. As there are no references to Buddhism in the *Gita* and there are a few archaic words and expressions, some of the greatest scholars have considered it pre-Buddhistic, i.e. about 500 BC. The Sanskrit of the *Bhagavad Gita* is, on the whole, simple and clear, like the oldest parts of the *Mahabharata*. This could be added as an argument for an early date; but the value of a spiritual scripture is its value to us here and now, and the real problem is how to translate its light into life.

The *Bhagavad Gita* is, above all, a spiritual poem and as such it must be judged; and it must be seen as a whole. An analytical approach will never reveal to us the full meaning of a poem.

If a Beethoven could give us in music the spirit of the *Bhagavad Gita*, what a wonderful symphony we should hear!

First of all come the stirring sounds of an impending battle, the great battle for an inner victory, and the despairing cry of the soul ready to give up the struggle. The soul is afraid of death: of the death of its passions and desires. It also fears the death of the body: is death the end of all? Then we hear the voice of the Eternal in man speaking to the soul that doubts and trembles: we hear about our immortality. After this come sounds infinitely serene and peaceful: the soul has peace from passions, and peace from fears and lower desires. The music becomes more urgent: it is the call to action, not action in time but action in Eternity: Karma Yoga. Those strains are followed by notes of eternal silence: it is vision, Jñana Yoga. Sweet human melodies are heard: it is the descent of Eternity into time, the incarnation of the divine. There is again a call to action, but this time the work is prayer, the deep prayer of silence which we find in Chapter 6. The music becomes more and more majestic: it is the revelation of God in all things in creation, but more evident in whatever is beautiful and good, in whatever has glory and power. Rising above the vast harmonies of this movement we hear a note of infinite tenderness. It is love. It is love that offers in adoration the whole of life to the God of Love, and God accepts the offering of a pure heart. The music rises again in tremendous crescendos that seem to overflow the limits of the universe: it is the vision of all things and of the whole universe in God. In this theme there is wonder and fear: the God of creation is also the God of destruction, the God of immortality is also the God of life and death.

After those ineffably sublime harmonies the music descends to softer melodies: it is the vision of God as man, as the friend of the struggling soul. Whatever we do for a human being we do it for Him.

For I was an hungered, and ye gave me meat: I was thirsty, and ye gave me drink: I was a stranger, and ye took me in: naked, and ye clothed me: I was sick, and ye visited me: I was in prison, and ye came unto me.   Matt. 25:35–6

The vast symphony of the *Bhagavad Gita* goes on. After the tenderness of love for Krishna, the God of Love, we have the universal harmonies of Brahman in the Universe. From the ONE in the many attained by love, we reach the splendour of all in the transcendent ONE. The music now changes: it is made of melodies of light and fire and darkness, the three Gunas, the three forces of the universe. New harmonies now are heard because we have the Tree of transmigration, the Tree of life, and the music carries us on from earth to heaven and from heaven to earth. We hear now terrible sounds: it is the noise of evil in creation; but this is drowned in the sounds of the good in all. The music returns now to earthly melodies, and after them we hear the glory of the sacred sounds OM, TAT, SAT: the Infinite beyond the beginning, the middle and the end of all our work.

At the end of this great symphony the different themes of the previous chapters are interwoven into one. The melodies of vision, love, and work in Eternity become one simple final strain of unearthly tenderness and beauty, the simple call of God to man: 'Come to me for thy salvation.'

This is the symphony of the *Bhagavad Gita*. There are in it several themes which rise above the rest. There is Yoga. It is obvious that the spiritual Yoga of the *Gita* is love; but Yoga also means 'Samadhi', a state of inner communion with the object of contemplation. When this contemplation is turned upon any being or object in creation, we have poetry: when it is turned towards the Source of all creation we have Light, spiritual vision. Inner Yoga is said to be above the Scriptures, because the Scriptures may be contradictory: above all past and future Scriptures the *Gita* places spiritual experience.

When thy mind leaves behind its dark forest of delusion, thou shalt go beyond the scriptures of times past and still to come.

When thy mind, that may be wavering in the contradictions of many scriptures, shall rest unshaken in divine contemplation, then the goal of Yoga is thine.   2.52–3

Spiritual experience is the only source of true spiritual faith, and this must never contradict reason, or as Shankara, c. AD 788–820, says in his commentary to the *Bhagavad Gita*: 'If a hundred scriptures should declare that fire is cold or that it is dark, we would suppose that they intend quite a different meaning from the apparent one!'

What is the indispensable condition for this spiritual experience? It is very simple, and it can be very difficult: it is the absence of desires. That is to say: if we want things as objects of possession we are in the lower region of 'having', but if we find in things objects of contemplation and inner communion we are in the higher region of 'being'. All true love is love of Eternity, and the inner Light of Being is revealed only when the clouds of becoming disappear. This is the meaning of the verse of the *Gita* that says: 'Even as all waters flow into the ocean, but the ocean never overflows, even so the sage feels desires, but he is ever one in his infinite peace' 2.70. Man can only find peace in the Infinite, not in the finite. This is expressed very clearly by St John of the Cross when he says: '*Cuando reparas en algo, dejas de arrojarte al Todo*', 'When you set your heart on anything, you cease to throw yourself into the All.' If we desire anything for its finite pleasure, we shall miss its infinite joy. The final words of Krishna to Arjuna are: 'Leave all things behind.' St John of the Cross tells us how we are able to leave all things behind and how not to look back: it is not to leave a vacuum in the soul, but to desire the Highest in all with the fire of burning love.

Prayer is described in the *Gita* as a means to achieve inner union. It is interesting to compare Chapter 6 of the *Gita* with this passage from St Peter of Alcántara, the teacher of St Teresa:

In meditation we consider carefully divine things, and we pass from one to another, so that the heart may feel love. It is as though we should strike a flint, and draw a spark of fire. But in contemplation the spark is struck: the love we were seeking is here. The soul enjoys silence and peace, not by many reasonings, but by simply contemplating the Truth.

When describing the state of the man who has found joy in God, the *Bhagavad Gita* says: 'When in recollection he withdraws all his senses from the attractions of the pleasures of sense, even as a tortoise withdraws all its limbs, then his is a serene wisdom' 2.58. St Teresa uses the same image when describing the prayer of recollection: 'I think I read somewhere that the soul is then like a tortoise or sea-urchin, which retreats into itself. Whoever said this no doubt understood what he was talking about.'

From the sense of harmony of the *Gita* comes its universal sympathy. This is suggested again and again through the whole poem, and it is definitely stated when Krishna says: 'In any way that men love me, in that same way they find my love' 4.11; and 'Even those who in faith worship other gods, because of their love they worship me' 9.23. This spirit of tolerance is expressed by St Teresa in her homely way when she advises her nuns against too much zeal: '*Ni hay para qué querer luego que todos vayan por nuestro camino*', 'There is no reason why we should want everyone else to follow our own path' Moradas 3.2.18.

The importance given to reason in the *Bhagavad Gita* is very great. Arjuna is told that he must seek salvation in reason, 2.49. And the first condition for a man to be worthy of God is that his reason should be pure – 18.51 and 18.57. Reason is the faculty given to man to distinguish true emotion from false emotionalism, faith from fanaticism, imagination from fancy, a true vision from a visionary illusion.

Self-harmony, or self-control, is praised again and again in the *Bhagavad Gita*. All perfection in action is a form of self-control, and this sense of perfection is the essence of the Karma Yoga of the *Gita*. The artist must have self-control in the moment of creation, and all work well done requires self-control; but the *Bhagavad Gita* wants us to transform our whole life into an act of creation. Only self-control makes it possible for us to live in harmony with other people. Of course, as Kant clearly shows, self-control must be at the service of a good will; but a good will must have power, and all virtue depends on the power of self-control.

The great psychological problem of self-control can be solved in different ways, and some are much easier than others. The spiritual answer is 'Seek ye first the kingdom of God.' If the joy of the inner kingdom is found, then the words of Spinoza, previously quoted, have found their spiritual setting. As soon the joy of the higher comes, the pleasure of the lower disappears.

Many are the themes of the symphony of the *Bhagavad Gita*, but the central ones are three: JÑANA, BHAKTI, and KARMA: Light, Love, and Life.

Jñana is the centre of the *Upanishads*, the means of reaching Brahman. The *Gita* also places the man of Jñana, the man of Light, above all men: he is in God. The three manifestations of Brahman revealed in Jñana are very present in the *Gita*: *Sat, Cit,* and *Ananda*: Being, Consciousness, and Joy.

Being can be felt in the silence of the soul. When an inner surrender of the self-conscious will takes place, there is great peace of mind and body, and gradually the movements of the mind seem to stop. There is no thinking, but there is a deep feeling of Being, of a deeper reality than the reality of ordinary consciousness. Faith in Being then becomes absolute: how could one doubt the deepest experience of one's life? Amiel describes glimpses of Being when he writes in his diary:

2nd January, 1880. Here there is a sense of rest and quietness. Silence in the house and outside. A tranquil fire gives a feeling of comfort.

The portrait of my mother seems to smile upon me. This peaceful morning makes me happy. Whatever pleasure we may get from our emotions I do not think it can equal those moments of silent peace which are glimpses of the joys of Paradise. Desire and fear, grief and anxiety are no more. We live a moment of life in the supreme region of our own being: pure consciousness. One feels an inner harmony free from the slightest agitation or tension. In those moments the state of the soul is solemn, perhaps akin to its condition beyond the grave. It is happiness as the Orientals understand it, the happiness of the hermit who is free from desire and struggle, and who simply adores in fullness of joy. We cannot find words to express this experience, because our languages can only describe particular and definite conditions of life: they have no words to express this silent contemplation, this heavenly quietness, this ocean of peace which both reflects the heavens above and is master of its own vast depth. Things return to their first principle, while memories become dreams of memories. The soul is then pure being and no longer feels its separation from the whole. It is conscious of the universal life, and at that moment is a centre of communion with God. It has nothing and it lacks nothing. Perhaps only the Yogis and the Sufis have known in its depth this condition of simple happiness which combines the joys of being and non-being, which is neither reflection nor will, and which is beyond the moral and the intellectual life: a return to oneness, to the fullness of things, the πλήρωμα, the vision of Plotinus and Proclus, the glad expectation of Nirvana.

This sense of Being is the sense of Brahman. From experiences similar to that described by Amiel, but of course infinitely greater, come the poems of St John of the Cross, the greatest spiritual poems of all time. In his aphorisms he says: 'In order to be All, do not desire to be anything. In order to know All, do not desire to know anything. In order to find the joy of All, do not desire to enjoy anything.' 'To be', 'to know', and 'to find joy' correspond to the SAT, CIT, ANANDA, 'Being, Consciousness, and Joy' of the *Upanishads*.

The great problem of the soul of man could then be expressed by the words of Hamlet which, as so often in Shakespeare, far transcend their context:

To be, or not to be – that is the question.

Whilst Jñana, the Light of God, is the highest theme in the *Bhagavad Gita* – 'The man of vision and I are one', 7.18, says Krishna – we find that it is Bhakti, love, which is the bond of union between man and God and therefore between man and man. We can read in the *Gita* words that sound like the words of Jesus: 'For this is my word of promise, that he who loves me shall not perish' 9.31. 'He who in this oneness of love, loves me in whatever he sees, wherever this man may live, in truth this man lives in me' 6.31. The *Bhagavad Gita* does not emphasize that God is reached by Jñana, because Jñana *is* God; but it says again and again that love is the means to reach God in whom Light and Love are one: 'By love he knows me in truth, who I am and what I am' 18.55 and 'Only by love can men see me, and know me, and come unto me' 11.54.

Socrates tells us that love is the messenger between the gods and man, and St John of the Cross says that 'It is love alone that unites the soul with God.' St Teresa in her homely way says 'What matters is not to think much, but to love much', '*No está la cosa en pensar mucho, sino en amar mucho*' although she adds that 'The love of God must not be built up in our imagination, but must be tried by works.' These ideas are in the spirit of the *Bhagavad Gita*. The vision of God is the grace of God; but the grace of God is the reward of the love of man.

We thus find in the *Bhagavad Gita* that love is interwoven with light.

Love is the power that moves the universe, the day of life, the night of death, and the new day after death. The radiance of this universe sends us a message of love and says that all creation came from love, that love impels evolution and that at the end of their time love returns all things to Eternity. Even as the rational mind can see that all matter is energy, the spirit can see that all energy is love, and everything in creation can be a mathematical equation for the mind and a song of love for the soul. Love leads to Light: Bhakti leads to Jñana, and Jñana is the joy of Brahman, the joy of the Infinite.

Our soul, like a bird in a cage, longs for the liberty of the vast air. We read the words of Pindar:

Things of a day! What are we, and what are we not? A dream about a shadow is man: yet, when some god-given splendour falls, a glory of light comes over him and his life is sweet.

The finite longs for the Infinite and we feel the sorrow of things that pass away; but beyond the tears of mankind there is the rainbow of joy. We can love the Infinite in all, and thus we can find joy in all, as it was so beautifully expressed in the *Brihad-Aranyaka Upanishad*:

It is not for the love of a husband that a husband is dear; but for the love of the Soul in the husband that a husband is dear.

It is not for the love of a wife that a wife is dear; but for the love of the Soul in the wife that a wife is dear.

It is not for the love of children that children are dear; but for the love of the Soul in children that children are dear.

It is not for the love of all that all is dear; but for the love of the Soul in all that all is dear.

The *Bhagavad Gita* is a book of Light and Love, but it is above all a book of Life: after Jñana and Bhakti, we have Karma.

The word Karma is connected with the Sanskrit root *Kri* which we find in the English words 'create' and 'creation'. Karma is work, and work is life. The word Karma means also 'sacred work' and is connected with the sacrifice of the *Vedas*: the ritual of religion. This meaning has to be considered in reading the *Gita*. Karma, work or action, is often contrasted in the *Bhagavad Gita* with Jñana, or contemplation: external ritual is set in contrast with inner spiritual life. This was the great spiritual change that took place in the *Upanishads*: from external ritual they went into inner life. This contrast is also found in the *Gita*, but in the *Gita* the word Karma has acquired a far deeper meaning, and this leads to one of the most sublime conceptions of man. All life is action, but every little finite action should be a surrender to the Infinite, even as breathing in seems to be the receiving of the gift of life, and the breathing out a surrender into the infinite Life. Every little work in life, however humble, can become an act of creation and therefore a means of salvation, because in all true creation we reconcile the finite with the Infinite, hence the joy of creation. When vision is pure and when creation is pure there is always joy.

Perhaps an example from Homer can help us to realize the conception of Karma in the *Bhagavad Gita*. In Book VI of the *Odyssey*, whilst Odysseus is sleeping in the shelter of the olive tree Nausicaa, the lovely daughter of the good ruler Alcinous, is gone with her maidens to the river to wash laundry, and Homer says:

In due course they reached the noble river with its never-failing pools, in which there was enough clear water always bubbling up and swirling by to clean the dirtiest clothes. Here they turned the mules loose from under the yoke and drove them along the eddying stream to graze on the sweet grass. Then they lifted the clothes by armfuls from the cart, dropped them into the dark water and trod them down briskly in the troughs, competing with each other in the work. When they had rinsed them till no dirt was left, they spread them out in a row along the sea-shore, just where the waves washed the shingle clean when they came tumbling up the beach. Next, after bathing and rubbing themselves with olive-oil, they took their meal at the riverside, waiting for the sunshine to dry the clothes.

And presently, when mistress and maids had all enjoyed their food, they threw off their headgear and began playing with a ball, while Nausicaa of the white arms led them in their song.

Translated by E. V. Rieu

Here we find the joy of vision and creation. The poet sees every action, however humble, under the radiance of eternal beauty, and we see the actors finding a pure joy in their work, as if they were working for Eternity. The poet sees things in an Eternity of beauty and joy, and the actors are doing their work beautifully, in the joy of Eternity. This is the spirit of Karma in the *Bhagavad Gita*. Nausicaa and her maidens were washing laundry for themselves and not for God; but they were in the joy of action, and therefore in the joy of God, the more so because they were unconscious of this greatness.

We find in Homer that work, even the most humble work, is beautiful. In the *Bhagavad Gita* we find that all work can be both beautiful and holy. We thus hear the words of Krishna: 'Offer to me all thy works and rest thy mind on the Supreme. Be free from vain hopes and selfish thoughts, and with inner peace fight thou thy fight' 3.30. And with a variation of the same idea: 'Whatever you do, or eat, or give, or offer in adoration, let it be an offering to me; and whatever you suffer, suffer it for me' 9.27. This is the same voice of St Paul to the Corinthians: 'Whether therefore ye eat, or drink, or whatsoever ye do, do all to the glory of God' 1 Cor. 10:31. And this work must be unselfish: 'Let the wise man work unselfishly for the good of all the world' *Gita* 3.25.

The praise of work as a means of salvation is later expressed in the poem and we hear that all men attain perfection when they find joy in their work, and they find joy in their work when their work is worship of God, because God is joy.

The greatness of the *Bhagavad Gita* is the greatness of the universe; but even as the wonder of the stars in heaven only reveals itself in the silence of the night, the wonder of this poem only reveals itself in the silence of the soul. We may begin when children to feel the mystery and wonder of this universe. One day, when very young, a few verses of the *Gita* may find their way into our hearts. We learn Sanskrit for the sake of the *Bhagavad Gita*. We read every translation we can find and compare different interpretations. We read the commentaries of Shankara and Ramanuja, histories of Indian philosophy and Sanskrit literature, and every publication on the *Bhagavad Gita* we can find. And far more than that: we may read the *Bhagavad Gita* in Sanskrit again and again, until we know the most important verses by heart, and chant them in Sanskrit, and the language of those verses becomes as familiar to us as our mother tongue. We may go to that poem in times of sorrow and joy and thus connect it with the deepest moments of our life; and write down the thoughts and emotions that the verses wake in us; and our reading may go on for years; and suddenly one day we may feel that we are reading the *Bhagavad Gita* for the first time. And why? Because new wonders have revealed themselves to us and we feel that the words of Arjuna are our own words: 'Speak to me again in full of thy power and of thy glory, for I am never tired, never, of hearing thy words of life' 10.18.

What is the essence of this great poem, what is the meaning of it all? The essence of the *Bhagavad Gita* is the vision of God in all things and of all things in God. It is the vision of Dante when he says in his *Paradiso*:

Nel suo profondo vidi che s'interna,
legato con amore in un volume,
ciò che per l'universo si squaderna.

La forma universal di questo nodo
creo ch'io vidi, perchè più di largo
dicendo questo, mi sento ch'io godo.

'Within its deep infinity I saw ingathered, and bound by love in one volume, the scattered leaves of all the universe.

'The universal form of this complex whole I think that I saw, because as I say this I feel my joy increasing.'

It is the vision of Arjuna in the *Bhagavad Gita*:

If the light of a thousand suns suddenly arose in the sky, that splendour might be compared to the radiance of the Supreme Spirit.

And Arjuna saw in that radiance the whole universe in its variety, standing in a vast unity in the body of the God of gods.   11.12–13

Love leads to Light, but the Light is not ours: it is given to us, it is given to us as a reward for our love and our good work. In the battle of the *Bhagavad Gita* there is a great symbol of hope: that he who has a good will and strives is never lost, and that in the battle for eternal life there can never be a defeat unless we run away from the battle.

The true progress of man on earth is the progress of an inner vision. We have a progress in science, but is it in harmony with a spiritual progress? We want a scientific progress, but do we want a moral progress? It is not enough to have more, or even to know more, but to live more, and if we want to live more we must love more. Love is 'the treasure hid in a field', and this field according to the *Gita* is our own soul. Here the treasure is found for which the wise merchant 'went and sold all he had'. And contrary to the law of matter where to give more means to have less, in the law of love the more one gives the more one has.

The spiritual visions of man confirm and illumine each other. We have the cosmic greatness of Hinduism, the moral issues of Zoroaster, the joy in Truth of Buddha, the spiritual victory of Jainism, the simple love of Tao, the wisdom of Confucius, the poetry of Shinto, the One God of Israel, the redeeming radiance of Christianity, the glory of God of Islam, the harmony of the Sikhs. Great poems in different languages have different values but they all are poetry, and the spiritual visions of man come all from One Light. In them we have Lamps of Fire that burn to the glory of God.

The finite in man longs for the Infinite. The love that moves the stars moves also the heart of man and a law of spiritual gravitation leads his soul to the Soul of the universe. Man sees the sun by the light of the sun, and he sees the Spirit by the light of his own inner spirit. The radiance of eternal beauty shines over this vast universe and in moments of contemplation we can see the Eternal in things that pass away. This is the message of the great spiritual seers; and all poetry and art and beauty is only an infinite variation of this message.

If we read the scriptures and books of wisdom of the world, if we consider the many spiritual experiences recorded in the writings of the past, we find one spiritual faith, and this faith is based on a vision of Truth. Not indeed the truth of the laws of nature gradually discovered by the human mind; but the Truth of our Being.

In the *Bhagavad Gita* we have faith, a faith based on spiritual vision. In this vision we have Light. Shall we see? This Song calls us to Love and Life. Shall we hear?

Every moment of our life can be the beginning of great things.

JUAN MASCARÓ

The Retreat,
Comberton, Cambridge
Christmas Day 1960

A NOTE ON THE
TRANSLATION

The aim of this translation is to give, without notes or
commentary, the spiritual message of the *Bhagavad Gita* in
pure English. In a few verses of the poem I have interwoven
one or more words to make clear the meaning, or to explain
a proper name, as when in 1.8 Karna is described as 'the
enemy of Arjuna, his half brother'.

Considering that 'the letter kills, but the spirit gives life',
I have avoided in a few cases the accepted translation of a
word. The most conspicuous example is the very first word
of the poem, 'Dharma', which I have in this particular case
translated by 'Truth'. I came to this conclusion after years of
thought; and I was very pleased when I read afterwards that
Rabindranath Tagore in his 'Sadhana', Chapter 4, says that
'Dharma' is 'the truth in us'. The words of a poem have
many waves of suggestion: I take the word 'Dharma' in this
case to mean the Truth of the universe.

As the *Gita* emphasizes God on earth more than the Brahman or Atman of the *Upanishads*, I have sometimes translated
the word Brahman or Atman by 'God'.

In rendering a verse I have most carefully considered all the
previous translations and interpretations I could find; but I
have followed my own light. Let us consider the words of
Isaiah, 30:15 'In returning and rest shall ye be saved; in
quietness and in confidence shall be your strength.' Moffat
translates 'Your safety lies in ceasing to make leagues, your

strength is quiet faith.' In the Authorized Version we not only have a meaning, in the context, that the words refer to a withdrawal from an alliance with Egypt: we have, far beyond this, a vast spiritual suggestion. Again, let us consider two versions which as prose mean very much the same, but how different is their poetical meaning! In Psalm 102 the Authorized Version says:

> I watch, and am
> As a sparrow alone upon the house top.

The scholars of the Revised Version tried to 'improve' upon the English of the Authorized Version by saying:

> I watch, and am become
> Like a sparrow that is alone upon the housetop.

By adding 'become' and 'that is' the music is broken, and the meaning is weakened because the music is broken: 'He that hath ears to hear, let him hear.'

I am responsible for the renderings in the Introduction, except for those which are signed.

As this translation was begun over twenty years ago and I have occasionally translated a verse up to twenty times before I was satisfied, I venture to hope that I have been true to the Spirit of the original and to myself. There is a verse in the *Bhagavad Gita*, 9.26, which sometimes came to my mind:

'He who offers to me with devotion only a leaf, or a flower, or a fruit, or even a little water, this I accept from that yearning soul, because with a pure heart it was offered with love.'

J.M.

THE
BHAGAVAD
GITA

I

1 On the field of Truth, on the battle-field of life, what came to pass, Sanjaya, when my sons and their warriors faced those of my brother Pandu?

SANJAYA

2 When your son Duryodhana saw the armies of the sons of Pandu he went to his master in the art of war and spoke to him these words:

3 See there, master, the vast army of the Pandavas well set in order of battle by the son of Drupada, your own wise pupil.

4 There can we see heroic warriors, powerful archers, as great as Bhima and Arjuna in battle: Yuyudhana and Virata and king Drupada of the great chariot of war.

5 And Dhrishta-ketu of the steadfast banner, and Chekitana, the king of the Chedis. We see the heroic king of Kasi, and Purujit the conqueror, and his brother Kunti-bhoja, and Saibya mighty among men.

6 And victorious Yudhamanyu, and powerful Uttamaujas; and Saubhadra, the son of Arjuna, and the five princes of queen Draupadi. See them all in their chariots of war.

7 But hear also the names of our greatest warriors, the

3

leaders of my own army. I will bring them to your memory.

8 There is yourself, my master in war, and also Bhishma, old and wise. There is Karna, the enemy of Arjuna, his half brother; and Kripa, victor of battles. There is your own son Asvatthama, and also my brother Vikarna. There is Saumadatti, king of the Bahikas.

9 And many other heroic warriors ready to give their lives for me; all armed with manifold weapons, and all of them masters of war.

10 We can number our armies led by Bhishma, but innumerable seem their armies led by Bhima.

11 Stand therefore all firm in the line of battle. Let us all defend our leader Bhishma.

12 To encourage Duryodhana, Bhishma, the glorious old warrior of the Kurus, sounded loud his war-cry like the roar of a lion, and then blew his far-sounding conch-shell.

13 Then the rumbling of war drums, the stirring sound of cymbals and trumpets, and the roaring of conch-shells and horns filled the sky with a fearful thunder.

14 Thereupon Krishna of Madhava and Arjuna, the son of Pandu, standing in their glorious chariot drawn by white horses, answered the challenge and blew their divine conch-shells.

15 Krishna, the Lord of the soul, blew his conch-shell Panchajanya. Arjuna, the winner of treasure, sounded forth his own Deva-datta. His brother Bhima, of tremendous feats, blew his great conch-shell the Paundra.

16 Their eldest brother, king Yudhishthira, sounded his Eternal-Victory; and Nakula and Sahadeva the Sweet-sounding and the Jewel-blossom.

17 And the king of Kasi of the powerful bow, and Sikhandi

of the great war chariot, Dhrishta-dyumna and Virata, and Satyaki the never-conquered;

18 And king Drupada and the sons of his daughter Draupadi; and Saubhadra, the heroic son of Arjuna, sounded from all sides their conch-shells of war.

19 At that fearful sound the earth and the heavens trembled, and also trembled the hearts of Duryodhana and his warriors.

20 The flight of arrows was now to begin and Arjuna, on whose banner was the symbol of an ape, saw Duryodhana and his warriors drawn up in their lines of battle. He thereupon took up his bow.

21 And spoke these words to Krishna:

ARJUNA

Drive my chariot, Krishna immortal, and place it between the two armies.

22 That I may see those warriors who stand there eager for battle, with whom I must now fight at the beginning of this war.

23 That I may see those who have come here eager and ready to fight, in their desire to do the will of the evil son of Dhrita-rashtra.

SANJAYA

24 When Krishna heard the words of Arjuna he drove their glorious chariot and placed it between the two armies.

25 And facing Bhishma and Drona and other royal rulers he said: 'See, Arjuna, the armies of the Kurus, gathered here on this field of battle.'

26 Then Arjuna saw in both armies fathers, grandfathers,

27 sons, grandsons; fathers of wives, uncles, masters;

28 brothers, companions and friends.

When Arjuna thus saw his kinsmen face to face in both lines of battle, he was overcome by grief and despair and thus he spoke with a sinking heart.

ARJUNA

When I see all my kinsmen, Krishna, who have come here on this field of battle,

29 Life goes from my limbs and they sink, and my mouth is sear and dry; a trembling overcomes my body, and my hair shudders in horror;

30 My great bow Gandiva falls from my hands, and the skin of my flesh is burning; I am no longer able to stand, because my mind is whirling and wandering.

31 And I see forebodings of evil, Krishna. I cannot foresee any glory if I kill my own kinsmen in the sacrifice of battle.

32 Because I have no wish for victory, Krishna, nor for a kingdom, nor for its pleasures. How can we want a kingdom, Govinda, or its pleasures or even life,

33 When those for whom we want a kingdom, and its pleasures, and the joys of life, are here in this field of battle about to give up their wealth and their life?

34 Facing us in the field of battle are teachers, fathers and sons; grandsons, grandfathers, wives' brothers; mothers' brothers and fathers of wives.

35 These I do not wish to slay, even if I myself am slain. Not even for the kingdom of the three worlds: how much less for a kingdom of the earth!

36 If we kill these evil men, evil shall fall upon us: what joy in their death could we have, O Janardana, mover of souls?

37 I cannot therefore kill my own kinsmen, the sons of king Dhrita-rashtra, the brother of my own father. What happiness could we ever enjoy, if we killed our own kinsmen in battle?

38 Even if they, with minds overcome by greed, see no evil in the destruction of a family, see no sin in the treachery to friends;

39 Shall we not, who see the evil of destruction, shall we not refrain from this terrible deed?

40 The destruction of a family destroys its rituals of righteousness, and when the righteous rituals are no more, unrighteousness overcomes the whole family.

41 When unrighteous disorder prevails, the women sin and are impure; and when women are not pure, Krishna, there is disorder of castes, social confusion.

42 This disorder carries down to hell the family and the destroyers of the family. The spirits of their dead suffer in pain when deprived of the ritual offerings.

43 Those evil deeds of the destroyers of a family, which cause this social disorder, destroy the righteousness of birth and the ancestral rituals of righteousness.

44 And have we not heard that hell is waiting for those whose familiar rituals of righteousness are no more?

45 O day of darkness! What evil spirit moved our minds when for the sake of an earthly kingdom we came to this field of battle ready to kill our own people?

46 Better for me indeed if the sons of Dhrita-rashtra, with arms in hand, found me unarmed, unresisting, and killed me in the struggle of war.

SANJAYA

47 Thus spoke Arjuna in the field of battle, and letting fall his bow and arrows he sank down in his chariot, his soul overcome by despair and grief.

2

1 Then arose the Spirit of Krishna and spoke to Arjuna, his friend, who with eyes filled with tears, thus had sunk into despair and grief.

KRISHNA

2 Whence this lifeless dejection, Arjuna, in this hour, the hour of trial? Strong men know not despair, Arjuna, for this wins neither heaven nor earth.

3 Fall not into degrading weakness, for this becomes not a man who is a man. Throw off this ignoble discouragement, and arise like a fire that burns all before it.

ARJUNA

4 I owe veneration to Bhishma and Drona. Shall I kill with my arrows my grandfather's brother, great Bhishma? Shall my arrows in battle slay Drona, my teacher?

5 Shall I kill my own masters who, though greedy of my kingdom, are yet my sacred teachers? I would rather eat in this life the food of a beggar than eat royal food tasting of their blood.

6 And we know not whether their victory or ours be better

for us. The sons of my uncle and king, Dhrita-rashtra, are here before us: after their death, should we wish to live?

7 In the dark night of my soul I feel desolation. In my self-pity I see not the way of righteousness. I am thy disciple, come to thee in supplication: be a light unto me on the path of my duty.

8 For neither the kingdom of the earth, nor the kingdom of the gods in heaven, could give me peace from the fire of sorrow which thus burns my life.

SANJAYA

9 When Arjuna the great warrior had thus unburdened his heart, 'I will not fight, Krishna,' he said, and then fell silent.

10 Krishna smiled and spoke to Arjuna – there between the two armies the voice of God spoke these words:

KRISHNA

11 Thy tears are for those beyond tears; and are thy words words of wisdom? The wise grieve not for those who live; and they grieve not for those who die – for life and death shall pass away.

12 Because we all have been for all time: I, and thou, and those kings of men. And we all shall be for all time, we all for ever and ever.

13 As the Spirit of our mortal body wanders on in childhood, and youth and old age, the Spirit wanders on to a new body: of this the sage has no doubts.

14 From the world of the senses, Arjuna, comes heat and comes cold, and pleasure and pain. They come and they go: they are transient. Arise above them, strong soul.

15 The man whom these cannot move, whose soul is one, beyond pleasure and pain, is worthy of life in Eternity.

16 The unreal never is: the Real never is not. This truth indeed has been seen by those who can see the true.

17 Interwoven in his creation, the Spirit is beyond destruction. No one can bring to an end the Spirit which is everlasting.

18 For beyond time he dwells in these bodies, though these bodies have an end in their time; but he remains immeasurable, immortal. Therefore, great warrior, carry on thy fight.

19 If any man thinks he slays, and if another thinks he is slain, neither knows the ways of truth. The Eternal in man cannot kill: the Eternal in man cannot die.

20 He is never born, and he never dies. He is in Eternity: he is for evermore. Never-born and eternal, beyond times gone or to come, he does not die when the body dies.

21 When a man knows him as never-born, everlasting, never-changing, beyond all destruction, how can that man kill a man, or cause another to kill?

22 As a man leaves an old garment and puts on one that is new, the Spirit leaves his mortal body and then puts on one that is new.

23 Weapons cannot hurt the Spirit and fire can never burn him. Untouched is he by drenching waters, untouched is he by parching winds.

24 Beyond the power of sword and fire, beyond the power of waters and winds, the Spirit is everlasting, omnipresent, never-changing, never-moving, ever One.

25 Invisible is he to mortal eyes, beyond thought and beyond change. Know that he is, and cease from sorrow.

26 But if he were born again and again, and again and again he were to die, even then, victorious man, cease thou from sorrow.

27 For all things born in truth must die, and out of death in truth comes life. Face to face with what must be, cease thou from sorrow.

28 Invisible before birth are all beings and after death invisible again. They are seen between two unseens. Why in this truth find sorrow?

29 One sees him in a vision of wonder, and another gives us words of his wonder. There is one who hears of his wonder; but he hears and knows him not.

30 The Spirit that is in all beings is immortal in them all: for the death of what cannot die, cease thou to sorrow.

31 Think thou also of thy duty and do not waver. There is no greater good for a warrior than to fight in a righteous war.

32 There is a war that opens the doors of heaven, Arjuna! Happy the warriors whose fate is to fight such war.

33 But to forgo this fight for righteousness is to forgo thy duty and honour: is to fall into transgression.

34 Men will tell of thy dishonour both now and in times to come. And to a man who is in honour, dishonour is more than death.

35 The great warriors will say that thou hast run from the battle through fear; and those who thought great things of thee will speak of thee in scorn.

36 And thine enemies will speak of thee in contemptuous words of ill-will and derision, pouring scorn upon thy courage. Can there be for a warrior a more shameful fate?

37 In death thy glory in heaven, in victory thy glory on earth. Arise therefore, Arjuna, with thy soul ready to fight.

38 Prepare for war with peace in thy soul. Be in peace in pleasure and pain, in gain and in loss, in victory or in the loss of a battle. In this peace there is no sin.

39 This is the wisdom of Sankhya – the vision of the Eternal.

Hear now the wisdom of Yoga, path of the Eternal and freedom from bondage.

40 No step is lost on this path, and no dangers are found. And even a little progress is freedom from fear.

41 The follower of this path has one thought, and this is the End of his determination. But many-branched and endless are the thoughts of the man who lacks determination.

42 There are men who have no vision, and yet they speak many words. They follow the letter of the Vedas, and they say: 'There is nothing but this.'

43 Their soul is warped with selfish desires, and their heaven is a selfish desire. They have prayers for pleasures and power, the reward of which is earthly rebirth.

44 Those who love pleasure and power hear and follow their words: they have not the determination ever to be one with the One.

45 The three Gunas of Nature are the world of the Vedas. Arise beyond the three Gunas, Arjuna! Be in Truth eternal, beyond earthly opposites. Beyond gains and possessions, possess thine own soul.

46 As is the use of a well of water where water everywhere overflows, such is the use of all the Vedas to the seer of the Supreme.

47 Set thy heart upon thy work, but never on its reward. Work not for a reward; but never cease to do thy work.

48 Do thy work in the peace of Yoga and, free from selfish desires, be not moved in success or in failure. Yoga is evenness of mind – a peace that is ever the same.

49 Work done for a reward is much lower than work done in the Yoga of wisdom. Seek salvation in the wisdom of reason. How poor those who work for a reward!

50 In this wisdom a man goes beyond what is well done and

what is not well done. Go thou therefore to wisdom:
Yoga is wisdom in work.

51 Seers in union with wisdom forsake the rewards of their
work, and free from the bonds of birth they go to the
abode of salvation.

52 When thy mind leaves behind its dark forest of delusion,
thou shalt go beyond the scriptures of times past and still
to come.

53 When thy mind, that may be wavering in the contradictions of many scriptures, shall rest unshaken in divine
contemplation, then the goal of Yoga is thine.

ARJUNA

54 How is the man of tranquil wisdom, who abides in divine
contemplation? What are his words? What is his silence?
What is his work?

KRISHNA

55 When a man surrenders all desires that come to the heart
and by the grace of God finds the joy of God, then his
soul has indeed found peace.

56 He whose mind is untroubled by sorrows, and for pleasures
he has no longings, beyond passion, and fear and anger, he
is the sage of unwavering mind.

57 Who everywhere is free from all ties, who neither rejoices
nor sorrows if fortune is good or is ill, his is a serene
wisdom.

58 When in recollection he withdraws all his senses from the
attractions of the pleasures of sense, even as a tortoise
withdraws all its limbs, then his is a serene wisdom.

59 Pleasures of sense, but not desires, disappear from the

austere soul. Even desires disappear when the soul has seen the Supreme.

60 The restless violence of the senses impetuously carries away the mind of even a wise man striving towards perfection.

61 Bringing them all into the harmony of recollection, let him sit in devotion and union, his soul finding rest in me. For when his senses are in harmony, then his is a serene wisdom.

62 When a man dwells on the pleasures of sense, attraction for them arises in him. From attraction arises desire, the lust of possession, and this leads to passion, to anger.

63 From passion comes confusion of mind, then loss of remembrance, the forgetting of duty. From this loss comes the ruin of reason, and the ruin of reason leads man to destruction.

64 But the soul that moves in the world of the senses and yet keeps the senses in harmony, free from attraction and aversion, finds rest in quietness.

65 In this quietness falls down the burden of all her sorrows, for when the heart has found quietness, wisdom has also found peace.

66 There is no wisdom for a man without harmony, and without harmony there is no contemplation. Without contemplation there cannot be peace, and without peace can there be joy?

67 For when the mind becomes bound to a passion of the wandering senses, this passion carries away man's wisdom, even as the wind drives a vessel on the waves.

68 The man who therefore in recollection withdraws his senses from the pleasures of sense, his is a serene wisdom.

69 In the dark night of all beings awakes to Light the tranquil

man. But what is day to other beings is night for the sage who sees.

70 Even as all waters flow into the ocean, but the ocean never overflows, even so the sage feels desires, but he is ever one in his infinite peace.

71 For the man who forsakes all desires and abandons all pride of possession and of self reaches the goal of peace supreme.

72 This is the Eternal in man, O Arjuna. Reaching him all delusion is gone. Even in the last hour of his life upon earth, man can reach the Nirvana of Brahman – man can find peace in the peace of his God.

3

1 If thy thought is that vision is greater than action, why dost thou enjoin upon me the terrible action of war?

2 My mind is in confusion because in thy words I find contradictions. Tell me in truth therefore by what path may I attain the Supreme.

KRISHNA

3 In this world there are two roads of perfection, as I told thee before, O prince without sin: Jñana Yoga, the path of wisdom of the Sankhyas, and Karma Yoga, the path of action of the Yogis.

4 Not by refraining from action does man attain freedom from action. Not by mere renunciation does he attain supreme perfection.

5 For not even for a moment can a man be without action. Helplessly are all driven to action by the forces born of Nature.

6 He who withdraws himself from actions, but ponders on their pleasures in his heart, he is under a delusion and is a false follower of the Path.

7 But great is the man who, free from attachments, and with a mind ruling its powers in harmony, works on the path of Karma Yoga, the path of consecrated action.

8 Action is greater than inaction: perform therefore thy task in life. Even the life of the body could not be if there were no action.

9 The world is in the bonds of action, unless the action is consecration. Let thy actions then be pure, free from the bonds of desire.

10 Thus spoke the Lord of Creation when he made both man and sacrifice: 'By sacrifice thou shalt multiply and obtain all thy desires.

11 'By sacrifice shalt thou honour the gods and the gods will then love thee. And thus in harmony with them shalt thou attain the supreme good.

12 'For pleased with thy sacrifice, the gods will grant to thee the joy of all thy desires. Only a thief would enjoy their gifts and not offer them in sacrifice.'

13 Holy men who take as food the remains of sacrifice become free from all their sins; but the unholy who have feasts for themselves eat food that is in truth sin.

14 Food is the life of all beings, and all food comes from rain above. Sacrifice brings the rain from heaven, and sacrifice is sacred action.

15 Sacred action is described in the Vedas and these come from the Eternal, and therefore is the Eternal everpresent in a sacrifice.

16 Thus was the Wheel of the Law set in motion, and that man lives indeed in vain who in a sinful life of pleasures helps not in its revolutions.

17 But the man who has found the joy of the Spirit and in the Spirit has satisfaction, who in the Spirit has found his peace, that man is beyond the law of action.

18 He is beyond what is done and beyond what is not done, and in all his works he is beyond the help of mortal beings.

19 In liberty from the bonds of attachment, do thou therefore the work to be done: for the man whose work is pure attains indeed the Supreme.

20 King Janaka and other warriors reached perfection by the path of action: let thy aim be the good of all, and then carry on thy task in life.

21 In the actions of the best men others find their rule of action. The path that a great man follows becomes a guide to the world.

22 I have no work to do in all the worlds, Arjuna – for these are mine. I have nothing to obtain, because I have all. And yet I work.

23 If I was not bound to action, never-tiring, everlastingly, men that follow many paths would follow my path of inaction.

24 If ever my work had an end, these worlds would end in destruction, confusion would reign within all: this would be the death of all beings.

25 Even as the unwise work selfishly in the bondage of selfish works, let the wise man work unselfishly for the good of all the world.

26 Let not the wise disturb the mind of the unwise in their selfish work. Let him, working with devotion, show them the joy of good work.

27 All actions take place in time by the interweaving of the forces of Nature; but the man lost in selfish delusion thinks that he himself is the actor.

28 But the man who knows the relation between the forces of Nature and actions, sees how some forces of Nature work upon other forces of Nature, and becomes not their slave.

29 Those who are under the delusion of the forces of Nature bind themselves to the work of these forces. Let not the wise man who sees the All disturb the unwise who sees not the All.

30 Offer to me all thy works and rest thy mind on the Supreme. Be free from vain hopes and selfish thoughts, and with inner peace fight thou thy fight.

31 Those who ever follow my doctrine and who have faith, and have a good will, find through pure work their freedom.

32 But those who follow not my doctrine, and who have ill-will, are men blind to all wisdom, confused in mind: they are lost.

33 'Even a wise man acts under the impulse of his nature: all beings follow nature. Of what use is restraint?'

34 Hate and lust for things of nature have their roots in man's lower nature. Let him not fall under their power: they are the two enemies in his path.

35 And do thy duty, even if it be humble, rather than another's, even if it be great. To die in one's duty is life: to live in another's is death.

ARJUNA

36 What power is it, Krishna, that drives man to act sinfully, even unwillingly, as if powerlessly?

KRISHNA

37 It is greedy desire and wrath, born of passion, the great evil, the sum of destruction: this is the enemy of the soul.

38 All is clouded by desire: as fire by smoke, as a mirror by dust, as an unborn babe by its covering.

39 Wisdom is clouded by desire, the everpresent enemy of the wise, desire in its innumerable forms, which like a fire cannot find satisfaction.

40 Desire has found a place in man's senses and mind and reason. Through these it blinds the soul, after having overclouded wisdom.

41 Set thou, therefore, thy senses in harmony, and then slay thou sinful desire, the destroyer of vision and wisdom.

42 They say that the power of the senses is great. But greater than the senses is the mind. Greater than the mind is Buddhi, reason; and greater than reason is He — the Spirit in man and in all.

43 Know Him therefore who is above reason; and let his peace give thee peace. Be a warrior and kill desire, the powerful enemy of the soul.

4

1 I revealed this everlasting Yoga to Vivasvan, the sun, the father of light. He in turn revealed it to Manu, his son, the father of man. And Manu taught his son, king Ikshvaku, the saint.

2 Then it was taught from father to son in the line of kings who were saints; but in the revolutions of times immemorial this doctrine was forgotten by men.

3 Today I am revealing to thee this Yoga eternal, this secret supreme: because of thy love for me, and because I am thy friend.

ARJUNA

4 Thy birth was after the birth of the sun: the birth of the sun was before thine. What is the meaning of thy words: 'I revealed this Yoga to Vivasvan'?

KRISHNA

5 I have been born many times, Arjuna, and many times hast thou been born. But I remember my past lives, and thou hast forgotten thine.

6 Although I am unborn, everlasting, and I am the Lord of

all, I come to my realm of nature and through my wondrous power I am born.

7 When righteousness is weak and faints and unrighteousness exults in pride, then my Spirit arises on earth.

8 For the salvation of those who are good, for the destruction of evil in men, for the fulfilment of the kingdom of righteousness, I come to this world in the ages that pass.

9 He who knows my birth as God and who knows my sacrifice, when he leaves his mortal body, goes no more from death to death, for he in truth comes to me.

10 How many have come to me, trusting in me, filled with my Spirit, in peace from passions and fears and anger, made pure by the fire of wisdom!

11 In any way that men love me, in that same way they find my love: for many are the paths of men, but they all in the end come to me.

12 Those who lust for early power offer sacrifice to the gods of the earth; for soon in this world of men success and power come from work.

13 The four orders of men arose from me, in justice to their natures and their works. Know that this work was mine, though I am beyond work, in Eternity.

14 In the bonds of works I am free, because in them I am free from desires. The man who can see this truth, in his work he finds his freedom.

15 This was known by men of old times, and thus in their work they found liberation. Do thou therefore thy work in life in the spirit that their work was done.

16 What is work? What is beyond work? Even some seers see this not aright. I will teach thee the truth of pure work, and this truth shall make thee free.

17 Know therefore what is work, and also know what is

wrong work. And know also of a work that is silence: mysterious is the path of work.

18 The man who in his work finds silence, and who sees that silence is work, this man in truth sees the Light and in all his works finds peace.

19 He whose undertakings are free from anxious desire and fanciful thought, whose work is made pure in the fire of wisdom: he is called wise by those who see.

20 In whatever work he does such a man in truth has peace: he expects nothing, he relies on nothing, and ever has fullness of joy.

21 He has no vain hopes, he is the master of his soul, he surrenders all he has, only his body works: he is free from sin.

22 He is glad with whatever God gives him, and he has risen beyond the two contraries here below; he is without jealousy, and in success or in failure he is one: his works bind him not.

23 He has attained liberation: he is free from all bonds, his mind has found peace in wisdom, and his work is a holy sacrifice. The work of such a man is pure.

24 Who in all his work sees God, he in truth goes unto God: God is his worship, God is his offering, offered by God in the fire of God.

25 There are Yogis whose sacrifice is an offering to the gods; but others offer as a sacrifice their own soul in the fire of God.

26 In the fire of an inner harmony some surrender their senses in darkness; and in the fire of the senses some surrender their outer light.

27 Others sacrifice their breath of life and also the powers of life in the fire of an inner union lighted by a flash of vision.

28 And others, faithful to austere vows, offer their wealth as a sacrifice, or their penance, or their practice of Yoga, or their sacred studies, or their knowledge.

29 Some offer their out-flowing breath into the breath that flows in; and the in-flowing breath into the breath that flows out: they aim at Pranayama, breath-harmony, and the flow of their breath is in peace.

30 Others, through practice of abstinence, offer their life into Life. All those know what is sacrifice, and through sacrifice purify their sins.

31 Neither this world nor the world to come is for him who does not sacrifice; and those who enjoy what remains of the sacrifice go unto Brahman.

32 Thus in many ways men sacrifice, and in many ways they go to Brahman. Know that all sacrifice is holy work, and knowing this thou shalt be free.

33 But greater than any earthly sacrifice is the sacrifice of sacred wisdom. For wisdom is in truth the end of all holy work.

34 Those who themselves have seen the Truth can be thy teachers of wisdom. Ask from them, bow unto them, be thou unto them a servant.

35 When wisdom is thine, Arjuna, never more shalt thou be in confusion; for thou shalt see all things in thy heart, and thou shalt see thy heart in me.

36 And even if thou wert the greatest of sinners, with the help of the bark of wisdom thou shalt cross the sea of evil.

37 Even as a burning fire burns all fuel into ashes, the fire of eternal wisdom burns into ashes all works.

38 Because there is nothing like wisdom which can make us pure on this earth. The man who lives in self-harmony finds this truth in his soul.

39 He who has faith has wisdom, who lives in self-harmony, whose faith is his life; and he who finds wisdom, soon finds the peace supreme.

40 But he who has no faith and no wisdom, and whose soul is in doubt, is lost. For neither this world, nor the world to come, nor joy is ever for the man who doubts.

41 He who makes pure his works by Yoga, who watches over his soul, and who by wisdom destroys his doubts, is free from the bondage of selfish work.

42 Kill therefore with the sword of wisdom the doubt born of ignorance that lies in thy heart. Be one in self-harmony, in Yoga, and arise, great warrior, arise.

5

1 Renunciation is praised by thee, Krishna, and then the Yoga of holy work. Of these two, tell me in truth, which is the higher path?

KRISHNA

2 Both renunciation and holy work are a path to the Supreme; but better than surrender of work is the Yoga of holy work.

3 Know that a man of true renunciation is he who craves not nor hates; for he who is above the two contraries soon finds his freedom.

4 Ignorant men, but not the wise, say that Sankhya and Yoga are different paths; but he who gives all his soul to one reaches the end of the two.

5 Because the victory won by the man of wisdom is also won by the man of good work. That man sees indeed the truth who sees that vision and creation are one.

6 But renunciation, Arjuna, is difficult to attain without Yoga of work. When a sage is one in Yoga he soon is one in God.

7 No work stains a man who is pure, who is in harmony, who is master of his life, whose soul is one with the soul of all.

8 'I am not doing any work,' thinks the man who is in
9 harmony, who sees the truth. For in seeing or hearing, smelling or touching, in eating or walking, or sleeping, or breathing, in talking or grasping or relaxing, and even in opening or closing his eyes, he remembers: 'It is the servants of my soul that are working.'

10 Offer all thy works to God, throw off selfish bonds, and do thy work. No sin can then stain thee, even as waters do not stain the leaf of the lotus.

11 The Yogi works for the purification of the soul: he throws off selfish attachment, and thus it is only his body or his senses or his mind or his reason that works.

12 This man of harmony surrenders the reward of his work and thus attains final peace: the man of disharmony, urged by desire, is attached to his reward and remains in bondage.

13 The ruler of his soul surrenders in mind all work, and rests in the joy of quietness in the castle of nine gates of his body: he neither does selfish work nor causes others to do it.

14 The Lord of the world is beyond the works of the world and their working, and beyond the results of these works; but the work of Nature rolls on.

15 The evil works or the good works of men are not his work. Wisdom is darkened by unwisdom, and this leads them astray.

16 But those whose unwisdom is made pure by the wisdom of their inner Spirit, their wisdom is unto them a sun and in its radiance they see the Supreme.

17 Their thoughts on Him and one with Him, they abide in Him, and He is the end of their journey. And they reach the land of never-returning, because their wisdom has made them pure of sin.

18 With the same evenness of love they behold a Brahmin who is learned and holy, or a cow, or an elephant, or a dog, and even the man who eats a dog.

19 Those whose minds are ever serene win the victory of life on this earth. God is pure and ever one, and ever one they are in God.

20 The man who sees Brahman abides in Brahman: his reason is steady, gone is his delusion. When pleasure comes he is not shaken, and when pain comes he trembles not.

21 He is not bound by things without, and within he finds inner gladness. His soul is one in Brahman and he attains everlasting joy.

22 For the pleasures that come from the world bear in them sorrows to come. They come and they go, they are transient: not in them do the wise find joy.

23 But he who on this earth, before his departure, can endure the storms of desire and wrath, this man is a Yogi, this man has joy.

24 He has inner joy, he has inner gladness, and he has found inner Light. This Yogi attains the Nirvana of Brahman: he is one with God and goes unto God.

25 Holy men reach the Nirvana of Brahman: their sins are no more, their doubts are gone, their soul is in harmony, their joy is in the good of all.

26 Because the peace of God is with them whose mind and soul are in harmony, who are free from desire and wrath, who know their own soul.

27 When the sage of silence, the Muni, ·closes the doors
28 of his soul and, resting his inner gaze between the eyebrows, keeps peaceful and even the ebbing and flowing of breath; and with life and mind and reason in harmony, and with desire and fear and wrath gone, keeps silent his soul before final freedom, he in truth has attained final freedom.

29 He knows me, the God of the worlds who accepts the offerings of men, the God who is the friend of all. He knows me and he attains peace.

ॐ

6

1 He who works not for an earthly reward, but does the work to be done, he is a Sanyasi, he is a Yogi: not he who lights not the sacred fire or offers not the holy sacrifice.

2 Because the Sanyasi of renunciation is also the Yogi of holy work; and no man can be a Yogi who surrenders not his earthly will.

3 When the sage climbs the heights of Yoga, he follows the path of work; but when he reaches the heights of Yoga, he is in the land of peace.

4 And he reaches the heights of Yoga when he surrenders his earthly will: when he is not bound by the work of his senses, and he is not bound by his earthly works.

5 Arise therefore! And with the help of thy Spirit lift up thy soul: allow not thy soul to fall. For thy soul can be thy friend, and thy soul can be thine enemy.

6 The soul of man is his friend when by the Spirit he has conquered his soul; but when a man is not lord of his soul then this becomes his own enemy.

7 When his soul is in peace he is in peace, and then his soul is in God. In cold or in heat, in pleasure or pain, in glory or disgrace, he is ever in Him.

8 When, happy with vision and wisdom, he is master of his own inner life, his soul sublime set on high, then he is called a Yogi in harmony. To him gold or stones or earth are one.

9 He has risen on the heights of his soul. And in peace he beholds relatives, companions and friends, those impartial or indifferent or who hate him: he sees them all with the same inner peace.

10 Day after day, let the Yogi practise the harmony of soul: in a secret place, in deep solitude, master of his mind, hoping for nothing, desiring nothing.

11 Let him find a place that is pure and a seat that is restful, neither too high nor too low, with sacred grass and a skin and a cloth thereon.

12 On that seat let him rest and practise Yoga for the purification of the soul: with the life of his body and mind in peace; his soul in silence before the One.

13 With upright body, head, and neck, which rest still and move not; with inner gaze which is not restless, but rests still between the eyebrows;

14 With soul in peace, and all fear gone, and strong in the vow of holiness, let him rest with mind in harmony, his soul on me, his God supreme.

15 The Yogi who, lord of his mind, ever prays in this harmony of soul, attains the peace of Nirvana, the peace supreme that is in me.

16 Yoga is a harmony. Not for him who eats too much, or for him who eats too little; not for him who sleeps too little, or for him who sleeps too much.

17 A harmony in eating and resting, in sleeping and keeping awake: a perfection in whatever one does. This is the Yoga that gives peace from all pain.

18 When the mind of the Yogi is in harmony and finds rest in

the Spirit within, all restless desires gone, then he is a Yukta, one in God.

19 Then his soul is a lamp whose light is steady, for it burns in a shelter where no winds come.

20 When the mind is resting in the stillness of the prayer of Yoga, and by the grace of the Spirit sees the Spirit and therein finds fulfilment;

21 Then the seeker knows the joy of Eternity: a vision seen by reason far beyond what senses can see. He abides therein and moves not from Truth.

22 He has found joy and Truth, a vision for him supreme. He is therein steady: the greatest pain moves him not.

23 In this union of Yoga there is liberty: a deliverance from the oppression of pain. This Yoga must be followed with faith, with a strong and courageous heart.

24 When all desires are in peace and the mind, withdrawing within, gathers the multitudinous straying senses into the harmony of recollection,

25 Then, with reason armed with resolution, let the seeker quietly lead the mind into the Spirit, and let all his thoughts be silence.

26 And whenever the mind unsteady and restless strays away from the Spirit, let him ever and for ever lead it again to the Spirit.

27 Thus joy supreme comes to the Yogi whose heart is still, whose passions are peace, who is pure from sin, who is one with Brahman, with God.

28 The Yogi who pure from sin ever prays in this harmony of soul soon feels the joy of Eternity, the infinite joy of union with God.

29 He sees himself in the heart of all beings and he sees all

beings in his heart. This is the vision of the Yogi of harmony, a vision which is ever one.

30 And when he sees me in all and he sees all in me, then I never leave him and he never leaves me.

31 He who in this oneness of love, loves me in whatever he sees, wherever this man may live, in truth this man lives in me.

32 And he is the greatest Yogi he whose vision is ever one: when the pleasure and pain of others is his own pleasure and pain.

ARJUNA

33 Thou hast told me of a Yoga of constant oneness, O Krishna, of a communion which is ever one. But, Krishna, the mind is inconstant: in its restlessness I cannot find rest.

34 The mind is restless, Krishna, impetuous, self-willed, hard to train: to master the mind seems as difficult as to master the mighty winds.

KRISHNA

35 The mind is indeed restless, Arjuna: it is indeed hard to train. But by constant practice and by freedom from passions the mind in truth can be trained.

36 When the mind is not in harmony, this divine communion is hard to attain; but the man whose mind is in harmony attains it, if he knows and if he strives.

ARJUNA

37 And if a man strives and fails and reaches not the End of Yoga, for his mind is not in Yoga; and yet this man has faith, what is his end, O Krishna?

38 Far from earth and far from heaven, wandering in the pathless winds, does he vanish like a cloud into air, not having found the path of God?

39 Be a light in my darkness, Krishna: be thou unto me a Light. Who can solve this doubt but thee?

KRISHNA

40 Neither in this world nor in the world to come does ever this man pass away; for the man who does the good, my son, never treads the path of death.

41 He dwells for innumerable years in the heaven of those who did good; and then this man who failed in Yoga is born again in the house of the good and the great.

42 He may even be born into a family of Yogis, where the wisdom of Yoga shines; but to be born in such a family is a rare event in this world.

43 And he begins his new life with the wisdom of a former life; and he begins to strive again, ever onwards towards perfection.

44 Because his former yearning and struggle irresistibly carries him onwards, and even he who merely yearns for Yoga goes beyond the words of books.

45 And thus the Yogi ever-striving, and with soul pure from sin, attains perfection through many lives and reaches the End Supreme.

46 Be thou a Yogi, Arjuna! Because the Yogi goes beyond those who only follow the path of the austere, or of wisdom, or of work.

47 And the greatest of all Yogis is he who with all his soul has faith, and he who with all his soul loves me.

7

1 Hear now, Arjuna, how thou shalt have the full vision of me, if thy heart is set on me and if, striving for Yoga, I am thy refuge supreme.

2 And I will speak to thee of that wisdom and vision which, when known, there is nothing else for thee to know.

3 Among thousands of men perhaps one strives for perfection; and among thousands of those who strive perhaps one knows me in truth.

4 The visible forms of my nature are eight: earth, water, fire, air, ether; the mind, reason, and the sense of 'I'.

5 But beyond my visible nature is my invisible Spirit. This is the fountain of life whereby this universe has its being.

6 All things have their life in this Life, and I am their beginning and end.

7 In this whole vast universe there is nothing higher than I. All the worlds have their rest in me, as many pearls upon a string.

8 I am the taste of living waters and the light of the sun and the moon. I am OM, the sacred word of the Vedas, sound in silence, heroism in men.

9 I am the pure fragrance that comes from the earth and the brightness of fire I am. I am the life of all living beings, and the austere life of those who train their souls.

10 And I am from everlasting the seed of eternal life. I am the intelligence of the intelligent. I am the beauty of the beautiful.

11 I am the power of those who are strong, when this power is free from passions and selfish desires. I am desire when this is pure, when this desire is not against righteousness.

12 And know that the three Gunas, the three states of the soul, come from me: peaceful light, restless life, and lifeless darkness. But I am not in them: they are in me.

13 How the whole world is under the delusion of these shadows of the soul, and knows not me though for ever I am!

14 My mysterious cloud of appearance is hard to pass beyond; but those who in truth come to me go beyond the world of shadows.

15 But men who do evil seek not me: their soul is darkened by delusion. Their vision is veiled by the cloud of appearance; their heart has chosen the path of evil.

16 There are four kinds of men who are good, and the four love me, Arjuna: the man of sorrows, the seeker of knowledge, the seeker of something he treasures, and the man of vision.

17 The greatest of these is the man of vision, who is ever one, who loves the One. For I love the man of vision, and the man of vision loves me.

18 These four kinds of men are good; but the man of vision and I are one. His whole soul is one in me, and I am his Path Supreme.

19 At the end of many lives the man of vision comes to me. 'God is all' this great man says. Such a spirit sublime how rarely is he found!

20 Men whose desires have clouded their vision, give their love to other gods, and led by their selfish nature, follow many other paths.

21 For if a man desires with faith to adore this or that god, I give faith unto that man, a faith that is firm and moves not.

22 And when this man, full of faith, goes and adores that god, from him he attains his desires; but whatever is good comes from me.

23 But these are men of little wisdom, and the good they want has an end. Those who love the gods go to the gods; but those who love me come unto me.

24 The unwise think that I am that form of my lower nature which is seen by mortal eyes: they know not my higher nature, imperishable and supreme.

25 For my glory is not seen by all: I am hidden by my veil of mystery; and in its delusion the world knows me not, who was never born and for ever I am.

26 I know all that was and is and is to come, Arjuna; but no one in truth knows me.

27 All beings are born in delusion, the delusion of division which comes from desire and hate.

28 But there are men who do what is good, and whose sins have come to an end. They are free from the delusion of division, and they worship me with all their soul.

29 For those who take refuge in me and strive to be free from age and death, they know Brahman, they know Atman, and they know what Karma is.

30 They know me in earth and in heaven, and in the fire of sacrifice. Their souls are pure, in harmony, and even when their time to go comes they see me.

8

1 Who is Brahman? Who is Atman? And what is Karma, Spirit Supreme? What is the kingdom of the earth? And what is the kingdom of Light?

2 Who offers the sacrifice in the body? How is the offering made? And when the time to go comes, how do those whose soul is in harmony know thee?

KRISHNA

3 Braham is the Supreme, the Eternal. Atman is his Spirit in man. Karma is the force of creation, wherefrom all things have their life.

4 Matter is the kingdom of the earth, which in time passes away; but the Spirit is the kingdom of Light. In this body I offer sacrifice, and my body is a sacrifice.

5 And he who at the end of his time leaves his body thinking of me, he in truth comes to my being: he in truth comes unto me.

6 For on whomsoever one thinks at the last moment of life, unto him in truth he goes, through sympathy with his nature.

7 Think of me therefore at all times; remember thou me and

fight. And with mind and reason on me, thou shalt in truth come to me.

8 For if a man thinks of the Spirit Supreme with a mind that wanders not, because it has been trained in Yoga, he goes to that Spirit of Light.

9 He who remembers the Poet, the Creator, who rules all
10 things from all time, smaller than the smallest atom, but upholding this vast universe, who shines like the sun beyond darkness, far far beyond human thought; and at the time of his departure is in union of love and the power of Yoga and, with a mind that wanders not, keeps the power of his life between his eyebrows, he goes to that Spirit Supreme, the Supreme Spirit of Light.

11 Hear now of that Path which the seers of the Veda call the Eternal, and which is reached by those who, in peace from earthly passions, live a life of holiness and strive for perfection.

12 If when a man leaves his earthly body he is in the silence of Yoga and, closing the doors of the soul, he keeps the mind in his heart, and places in the head the breath of life.

13 And remembering me he utters OM, the eternal WORD of Brahman, he goes to the Path Supreme.

14 Those who in the devotion of Yoga rest all their soul ever on me, very soon come unto me.

15 And when those great spirits are in me, the Abode of joy supreme, they never return again to this world of human sorrow.

16 For all the worlds pass away, even the world of Brahma, the Creator: they pass away and return. But he who comes unto me goes no more from death to death.

17 They who know that the vast day of Brahma, the god of

creation, ever lasts a thousand ages; and that his night lasts also a thousand ages – they know in truth day and night.

18 When that day comes, all the visible creation arises from the Invisible; and all creation disappears into the Invisible when the night of darkness comes.

19 Thus the infinity of beings which live again and again all powerlessly disappear when the night of darkness comes; and they all return again at the rising of the day.

20 But beyond this creation, visible and invisible, there is an Invisible, higher, Eternal; and when all things pass away this remains for ever and ever.

21 This Invisible is called the Everlasting and is the highest End supreme. Those who reach him never return. This is my supreme abode.

22 This Spirit Supreme, Arjuna, is attained by an ever-living love. In him all things have their life, and from him all things have come.

23 Hear now of a time of light when Yogis go to eternal Life; and hear of a time of darkness when they return to death on earth.

24 If they depart in the flame, the light, the day, the bright weeks of the moon and the months of increasing light of the sun, those who know Brahman go unto Brahman.

25 But if they depart in the smoke, the night, the dark weeks of the moon and the months of decreasing days of the sun, they enter the lunar light, and return to the world of death.

26 These are the two paths that are for ever: the path of light and the path of darkness. The one leads to the land of never-returning: the other returns to sorrow.

27 The Yogi who knows these two paths lives nevermore in

delusion. Therefore ever and for ever be thou one in Yoga, Arjuna.

28 There is a reward that comes from the Vedas, or from sacrifice, from an austere life or from holy gifts. But a far greater reward is attained by the Yogi who knows the truth of Light and darkness: he attains his Everlasting Home.

9

1 I will tell thee a supreme mystery, because thy soul has faith. It is vision and wisdom and when known thou shalt be free from sin.

2 It is the supreme mystery and wisdom and the purification supreme. Seen in a wonder of vision, it is a path of righteousness very easy to follow, leading to the highest End.

3 But those who have no faith in this Truth, come not unto me: they return to the cycles of life in death.

4 All this visible universe comes from my invisible Being. All beings have their rest in me, but I have not my rest in them.

5 And in truth they rest not in me: consider my sacred mystery. I am the source of all beings, I support them all, but I rest not in them.

6 Even as the mighty winds rest in the vastness of the ethereal space, all beings have their rest in me. Know thou this truth.

7 At the end of the night of time all things return to my nature; and when the new day of time begins I bring them again into light.

8 Thus through my nature I bring forth all creation, and this rolls round in the circles of time.

9 But I am not bound by this vast work of creation. I am and I watch the drama of works.

10 I watch and in its work of creation nature brings forth all that moves and moves not: and thus the revolutions of the world go round.

11 But the fools of the world know not me when they see me in my own human body. They know not my Spirit supreme, the infinite God of this all.

12 Their hope is in vain, their works are in vain, their learning is vain, their thoughts are vain. They fall down to the nature of demons, towards the darkness of delusion of hell.

13 But there are some great souls who know me: their refuge is my own divine nature. They love me with a oneness of love: they know that I am the source of all.

14 They praise me with devotion, they praise me for ever and ever. Their vows are strong; their harmony is ever one; and they worship me with their love.

15 Others worship me, and work for me, with the sacrifice of spiritual vision. They worship me as One and as many, because they see that all is in me.

16 For I am the sacrifice and the offering, the sacred gift and the sacred plant. I am the holy words, the holy food, the holy fire, and the offering that is made in the fire.

17 I am the Father of this universe, and even the Source of the Father. I am the Mother of this universe, and the Creator of all. I am the Highest to be known, the Path of purification, the holy OM, the Three Vedas.

18 I am the Way, and the Master who watches in silence; thy friend and thy shelter and thy abode of peace. I am the beginning and the middle and the end of all things: their seed of Eternity, their Treasure supreme.

19 The heat of the sun comes from me, and I send and

withhold the rain. I am life immortal and death; I am what is and I am what is not.

20 There are men who know the Three Vedas, who drink the Soma, who are pure from sin. They worship and pray for heaven. They reach indeed the heaven of Indra, the king of the gods, and there they enjoy royal pleasures.

21 They enjoy that vast world of heaven, but the reward of their work comes to an end: they return to the world of death. They follow the words of the Three Vedas, they lust for pleasures that pass away: in truth they attain pleasures that pass away.

22 But to those who adore me with a pure oneness of soul, to those who are ever in harmony, I increase what they have and I give them what they have not.

23 Even those who in faith worship other gods, because of their love they worship me, although not in the right way.

24 For I accept every sacrifice, and I am their Lord supreme. But they know not my pure Being, and because of this they fall.

25 For those who worship the gods go to the gods, and those who worship the fathers go to the fathers. Those who worship the lower spirits go to the lower spirits; but those who worship me come unto me.

26 He who offers to me with devotion only a leaf, or a flower, or a fruit, or even a little water, this I accept from that yearning soul, because with a pure heart it was offered with love.

27 Whatever you do, or eat, or give, or offer in adoration, let it be an offering to me; and whatever you suffer, suffer it for me.

28 Thus thou shalt be free from the bonds of Karma which

yield fruits that are evil and good; and with thy soul one in renunciation thou shalt be free and come to me.

29 I am the same to all beings, and my love is ever the same; but those who worship me with devotion, they are in me and I am in them.

30 For even if the greatest sinner worships me with all his soul, he must be considered righteous, because of his righteous will.

31 And he shall soon become pure and reach everlasting peace. For this is my word of promise, that he who loves me shall not perish.

32 For all those who come to me for shelter, however weak or humble or sinful they may be – women or Vaisyas or Sudras – they all reach the Path supreme.

33 How much more the holy Brahmins and the royal saints who love me! Having come to this world of sorrow, which is transient, love thou me.

34 Give me thy mind and give me thy heart, give me thy offerings and thy adoration; and thus with thy soul in harmony, and making me thy goal supreme, thou shalt in truth come to me.

10

1 Hear again mighty Arjuna, hear the glory of my Word again. I speak for thy true good, because thy heart finds joy in me.

2 The hosts of the gods know not my birth, nor the great seers on earth, for all the gods come from me, and all the great seers, all.

3 He who knows I am beginningless, unborn, the Lord of all the worlds, this mortal is free from delusion, and from all evils he is free.

4 Intelligence, spiritual vision, victory over delusion,

5 patient forgiveness, truth, self-harmony, peacefulness, joys and sorrows, to be and not to be, fear and freedom from fear, harmlessness and non-violence, an everquietness, satisfaction, simple austerity, generosity, honour and dishonour: these are the conditions of mortals and they all arise from me.

6 The seven seers of times immemorial, and the four founders of the human race, being in me, came from my mind; and from them came this world of men.

7 He who knows my glory and power, he has the oneness of unwavering harmony. This is my truth.

8 I am the One source of all: the evolution of all comes from

me. The wise think this and they worship me in adoration of love.

9 Their thoughts are on me, their life is in me, and they give light to each other. For ever they speak of my glory; and they find peace and joy.

10 To those who are ever in harmony, and who worship me with their love, I give the Yoga of vision and with this they come to me.

11 In my mercy I dwell in their hearts and I dispel their darkness of ignorance by the light of the lamp of wisdom.

ARJUNA

12 Supreme Brahman, Light supreme, and supreme purification, Spirit divine eternal, unborn God from the beginning, omnipresent Lord of all.

13 Thus all the seers praised thee: the seer divine Narada; Asita, Devala and Vyasa. And this is now thy revelation.

14 I have faith in all thy words, because these words are words of truth, and neither the gods in heaven nor the demons in hell can grasp thy infinite vastness.

15 Only thy Spirit knows thy Spirit: only thou knowest thyself. Source of Being in all beings, God of gods, ruler of all.

16 Tell me in thy mercy of thy divine glory wherein thou art ever, and all the worlds are.

17 For ever in meditation, how shall I ever know thee? And in what manifestations shall I think of thee, my Lord?

18 Speak to me again in full of thy power and of thy glory, for I am never tired, never, of hearing thy words of life.

KRISHNA

19 Listen and I shall reveal to thee some manifestations of my divine glory. Only the greatest, Arjuna, for there is no end to my infinite greatness.

20 I am the soul, prince victorious, which dwells in the heart of all things. I am the beginning, the middle, and the end of all that lives.

21 Among the sons of light I am Vishnu, and of luminaries the radiant sun. I am the lord of the winds and storms, and of the lights in the night I am the moon.

22 Of the Vedas I am the Veda of songs, and I am Indra, the chief of the gods. Above man's senses I am the mind, and in all living beings I am the light of consciousness.

23 Among the terrible powers I am the god of destruction; and among monsters Vittesa, the lord of wealth. Of radiant spirits I am fire; and among high mountains the mountain of the gods.

24 Of priests I am the divine priest Brihaspati, and among warriors Skanda, the god of war. Of lakes I am the vast ocean.

25 Among great seers I am Bhrigu; and of words I am OM, the Word of Eternity. Of prayers I am the prayer of silence; and of things that move not I am the Himalayas.

26 Of trees I am the tree of life, and of heavenly seers Narada. Among celestial musicians, Chitra-ratha; and among seers on earth, Kapila.

27 Of horses I am the horse of Indra, and of elephants his elephant Airavata. Among men I am king of men.

28 Of weapons I am the thunderbolt, and of cows the cow of wonder. Among creators I am the creator of love; and among serpents the serpent of Eternity.

29 Among the snakes of mystery I am Ananta, and of those born in the waters I am Varuna, their lord. Of the spirits of the fathers I am Aryaman, and of rulers Yama, the ruler of death.

30 Of demons I am Prahlada their prince, and of all things that measure I am time. Of beasts I am the king of beasts, and of birds Vainateya who carries a god.

31 Among things of purification I am the wind, and among warriors I am Rama, the hero supreme. Of fishes in the sea I am Makara the wonderful, and among all rivers the holy Ganges.

32 I am the beginning and the middle and the end of all that is. Of all knowledge I am the knowledge of the Soul. Of the many paths of reason I am the one that leads to Truth.

33 Of sounds I am the first sound, A; of compounds I am coordination. I am time, never-ending time. I am the Creator who sees all.

34 I am death that carries off all things, and I am the source of things to come. Of feminine nouns I am Fame and Prosperity; Speech, Memory and Intelligence; Constancy and patient Forgiveness.

35 I am the Brihat songs of all songs in the Vedas. I am the Gayatri of all measures in verse. Of months I am the first of the year, and of the seasons the season of flowers.

36 I am the cleverness in the gambler's dice. I am the beauty of all things beautiful. I am victory and the struggle for victory. I am the goodness of those who are good.

37 Of the children of Vrishni I am Krishna; and of the sons of Pandu I am Arjuna. Among seers in silence I am Vyasa; and among poets the poet Usana.

38 I am the sceptre of the rulers of men; and I am the wise policy of those who seek victory. I am the silence of

hidden mysteries; and I am the knowledge of those who know.

39 And know, Arjuna, that I am the seed of all things that are; and that no being that moves or moves not can ever be without me.

40 There is no end of my divine greatness, Arjuna. What I have spoken here to thee shows only a small part of my infinity.

41 Know thou that whatever is beautiful and good, whatever has glory and power is only a portion of my own radiance.

42 But of what help is it to thee to know this diversity? Know that with one single fraction of my Being I pervade and support the Universe, and know that I AM.

11

1 In thy mercy thou hast told me the secret supreme of thy Spirit, and thy words have dispelled my delusion.

2 I have heard in full from thee of the coming and going of beings, and also of thy infinite greatness.

3 I have heard thy words of truth, but my soul is yearning to see: to see thy form as God of this all.

4 If thou thinkest, O my Lord, that it can be seen by me, show me, O God of Yoga, the glory of thine own Supreme Being.

KRISHNA

5 By hundreds and then by thousands, behold, Arjuna, my manifold celestial forms of innumerable shapes and colours.

6 Behold the gods of the sun, and those of fire and light; the gods of storm and lightning, and the two luminous charioteers of heaven. Behold, descendant of Bharata, marvels never seen before.

7 See now the whole universe with all things that move and move not, and whatever thy soul may yearn to see. See it all as One in me.

8 But thou never canst see me with these thy mortal eyes: I will give thee divine sight. Behold my wonder and glory.

SANJAYA

9 When Krishna, the God of Yoga, had thus spoken, O king, he appeared then to Arjuna in his supreme divine form.

10 And Arjuna saw in that form countless visions of wonder: eyes from innumerable faces, numerous celestial ornaments, numberless heavenly weapons;

11 Celestial garlands and vestures, forms anointed with heavenly perfumes. The Infinite Divinity was facing all sides, all marvels in him containing.

12 If the light of a thousand suns suddenly arose in the sky, that splendour might be compared to the radiance of the Supreme Spirit.

13 And Arjuna saw in that radiance the whole universe in its variety, standing in a vast unity in the body of the God of gods.

14 Trembling with awe and wonder, Arjuna bowed his head, and joining his hands in adoration he thus spoke to his God.

ARJUNA

15 I see in thee all the gods, O my God; and the infinity of the beings of thy creation. I see god Brahma on his throne of lotus, and all the seers and serpents of light.

16 All around I behold thy Infinity: the power of thy innumerable arms, the visions from thy innumerable eyes, the words from thy innumerable mouths, and the fire of life of thy innumerable bodies. Nowhere I see a beginning or middle or end of thee, O God of all, Form Infinite!

17 I see the splendour of an infinite beauty which illumines the whole universe. It is thee! with thy crown and sceptre and circle. How difficult thou art to see! But I see thee: as fire, as the sun, blinding, incomprehensible.

18 Thou art the Imperishable, the highest End of knowledge, the support of this vast universe. Thou, the everlasting ruler of the law of righteousness, the Spirit who is and who was at the beginning.

19 I see thee without beginning, middle, or end; I behold thy infinite power, the power of thy innumerable arms. I see thine eyes as the sun and the moon. And I see thy face as a sacred fire that gives light and life to the whole universe in the splendour of a vast offering.

20 Heaven and earth and all the infinite spaces are filled with thy Spirit; and before the wonder of thy fearful majesty the three worlds tremble.

21 The hosts of the gods come to thee and, joining palms in awe and wonder, they praise and adore. Sages and saints come to thee, and praise thee with songs of glory.

22 The Rudras of destruction, the Vasus of fire, the Sadhyas of prayers, the Adityas of the sun; the lesser gods Visve-Devas, the two Asvins charioteers of heaven, the Maruts of winds and storms, the Ushmapas spirits of ancestors; the celestial choirs of Gandharvas, the Yakshas keepers of wealth, the demons of hell and the Siddhas who on earth reached perfection: they all behold thee with awe and wonder.

23 But the worlds also behold thy fearful mighty form, with many mouths and eyes, with many bellies, thighs and feet, frightening with terrible teeth: they tremble in fear, and I also tremble.

24 When I see thy vast form, reaching the sky, burning with many colours, with wide open mouths, with vast flaming eyes, my heart shakes in terror: my power is gone and gone is my peace, O Vishnu!

25 Like the fire at the end of Time which burns all in the last day, I see thy vast mouths and thy terrible teeth. Where am I? Where is my shelter? Have mercy on me, God of gods, Refuge Supreme of the world!

26 The sons of Dhrita-rashtra, all of them, with other
27 princes of this earth, and Bhishma and Drona and great Karna, and also the greatest warriors of our host, all enter rushing into thy mouths, terror-inspiring with their fearful fangs. Some are caught between them, and their heads crushed into powder.

28 As roaring torrents of waters rush forward into the ocean, so do these heroes of our mortal world rush into thy flaming mouths.

29 And as moths swiftly rushing enter a burning flame and die, so all these men rush to thy fire, rush fast to their own destruction.

30 The flames of thy mouths devour all the worlds. Thy glory fills the whole universe. But how terrible thy splendours burn!

31 Reveal thyself to me! Who art thou in this form of terror? I adore thee, O god supreme: be gracious unto me. I yearn to know thee, who art from the beginning: for I understand not thy mysterious works.

KRISHNA

32 I am all-powerful Time which destroys all things, and I have come here to slay these men. Even if thou dost not fight, all the warriors facing thee shall die.

33 Arise therefore! Win thy glory, conquer thine enemies, and enjoy thy kingdom. Through the fate of their Karma I

have doomed them to die: be thou merely the means of my work.

34 Drona, Bhishma, Jayad-ratha and Karna, and other heroic warriors of this great war have already been slain by me: tremble not, fight and slay them. Thou shalt conquer thine enemies in battle.

SANJAYA

35 When Arjuna heard the words of Krishna he folded his hands trembling; and with a faltering voice, and bowing in adoration, he spoke.

ARJUNA

36 It is right, O God, that peoples sing thy praises, and that they are glad and rejoice in thee. All evil spirits fly away in fear; but the hosts of the saints bow down before thee.

37 How could they not bow down in love and adoration, before thee, God of gods, Spirit Supreme? Thou creator of Brahma, the god of creation, thou infinite, eternal, refuge of the world! Thou who art all that is, and all that is not, and all that is Beyond.

38 Thou God from the beginning, God in man since man was. Thou Treasure supreme of this vast universe. Thou the One to be known and the Knower, the final resting place. Thou infinite Presence in whom all things are.

39 God of the winds and the waters, of fire and death! Lord of the solitary moon, the Creator, the Ancestor of all! Adoration unto thee, a thousand adorations; and again and again unto thee adoration.

40 Adoration unto thee who art before me and behind me: adoration unto thee who art on all sides, God of all. All-

powerful God of immeasurable might. Thou art the consummation of all: thou art all.

41 If in careless presumption, or even in friendliness, I said 'Krishna! Son of Yadu! My friend!', this I did unconscious of thy greatness.

42 And if in irreverence I was disrespectful — when alone or with others — and made a jest of thee at games, or resting, or at a feast, forgive me in thy mercy, O thou Immeasurable!

43 Father of all. Master supreme. Power supreme in all the worlds. Who is like thee? Who is beyond thee?

44 I bow before thee, I prostrate in adoration; and I beg thy grace, O glorious Lord! As a father to his son, as a friend to his friend, as a lover to his beloved, be gracious unto me, O God.

45 In a vision I have seen what no man has seen before: I rejoice in exultation, and yet my heart trembles with fear. Have mercy upon me, Lord of gods, Refuge of the whole universe: show me again thine own human form.

46 I yearn to see thee again with thy crown and sceptre and circle. Show thyself to me again in thine own four-armed form, thou of arms infinite, Infinite Form.

KRISHNA

47 By my grace and my wondrous power I have shown to thee, Arjuna, this form supreme made of light, which is the Infinite, the All: mine own form from the beginning, never seen by man before.

48 Neither Vedas, nor sacrifices, nor studies, nor benefactions, nor rituals, nor fearful austerities can give the vision of my Form Supreme. Thou alone hast seen this Form, thou the greatest of the Kurus.

49 Thou hast seen the tremendous form of my greatness, but fear not, and be not bewildered. Free from fear and with a glad heart see my friendly form again.

SANJAYA

50 Thus spoke Vasudeva to Arjuna, and revealed himself in his human form. The God of all gave peace to his fears and showed himself in his peaceful beauty.

ARJUNA

51 When I see thy gentle human face, Krishna, I return to my own nature, and my heart has peace.

KRISHNA

52 Thou hast seen now face to face my form divine so hard to see: for even the gods in heaven ever long to see what thou hast seen.

53 Not by the Vedas, or an austere life, or gifts to the poor, or ritual offerings can I be seen as thou hast seen me.

54 Only by love can men see me, and know me, and come unto me.

55 He who works for me, who loves me, whose End Supreme I am, free from attachment to all things, and with love for all creation, he in truth comes unto me.

12

ARJUNA

1 Those who in oneness worship thee as God immanent in all; and those who worship the Transcendent, the Imperishable – Of these, who are the best Yogis?

KRISHNA

2 Those who set their hearts on me and ever in love worship me, and who have unshakeable faith, these I hold as the best Yogis.

3 But those who worship the Imperishable, the Infinite, the Transcendent unmanifested; the Omnipresent, the Beyond all thought, the Immutable, the Never-changing, the Ever One;

4 Who have all the powers of their soul in harmony, and the same loving mind for all; who find joy in the good of all beings – they reach in truth my very self.

5 Yet greater is the toil of those whose minds are set on the Transcendent, for the path of the Transcendent is hard for mortals to attain.

6 But they for whom I am the End Supreme, who surrender
7 all their works to me, and who with pure love meditate on me and adore me – these I very soon deliver from the ocean of death and life-in-death, because they have set their heart on me.

8 Set thy heart on me alone, and give to me thy understanding: thou shalt in truth live in me hereafter.

9 But if thou art unable to rest thy mind on me, then seek to reach me by the practice of Yoga concentration.

10 If thou art not able to practise concentration, consecrate all thy work to me. By merely doing actions in my service thou shalt attain perfection.

11 And if even this thou art not able to do, then take refuge in devotion to me and surrender to me the fruit of all thy work — with the selfless devotion of a humble heart.

12 For concentration is better than mere practice, and meditation is better than concentration; but higher than meditation is surrender in love of the fruit of one's actions, for on surrender follows peace.

13 The man who has a good will for all, who is friendly and has compassion; who has no thoughts of 'I' or 'mine', whose peace is the same in pleasures and sorrows, and who is forgiving;

14 This Yogi of union, ever full of my joy, whose soul is in harmony and whose determination is strong; whose mind and inner vision are set on me — this man loves me, and he is dear to me.

15 He whose peace is not shaken by others, and before whom other people find peace, beyond excitement and anger and fear — he is dear to me.

16 He who is free from vain expectations, who is pure, who is wise and knows what to do, who in inner peace watches both sides, who shakes not, who works for God and not for himself — this man loves me, and he is dear to me.

17 He who feels neither excitement nor repulsion, who complains not and lusts not for things; who is beyond good and evil, and who has love — he is dear to me.

18 The man whose love is the same for his enemies or his friends, whose soul is the same in honour or disgrace, who is beyond heat or cold or pleasure or pain, who is free from the chains of attachments;

19 Who is balanced in blame and in praise, whose soul is silent, who is happy with whatever he has, whose home is not in this world, and who has love – this man is dear to me.

20 But even dearer to me are those who have faith and love, and who have me as their End Supreme: those who hear my words of Truth, and who come to the waters of Everlasting Life.

13

KRISHNA

1 This body, Arjuna, is called the field. He who knows this is called the knower of the field.

2 Know that I am the knower in all the fields of my creation; and that the wisdom which sees the field and the knower of the field is true wisdom.

3 Hear from me briefly what the field is and how it is, what its changes are and whence each one comes; who is the knower and what is his power.

4 This has been sung by seers of the Vedas in many musical measures of verse; and in great words about Brahman, words of faith and full of truth.

5 The five elements, the thought of 'I', consciousness, subconsciousness, the five powers of feeling and the five of action, the one mind over them, the five fields of sense-perception;

6 Desire, aversion, pleasure, pain, the power of mental unification, intelligence, and courage: this is the field and its modifications.

7 Humbleness, sincerity, harmlessness, forgiveness, uprightness, devotion to the spiritual master, purity, steadiness, self-harmony;

8 Freedom from the lust of the senses, absence of the thought

of 'I', perception of the sorrows of birth, death, old age, disease, and suffering;

9 Freedom from the chains of attachments, even from a selfish attachment to one's children, wife, or home; an ever-present evenness of mind in pleasant or unpleasant events;

10 A single oneness of pure love, of never-straying love for me; retiring to solitary places, and avoiding the noisy multitudes;

11 A constant yearning to know the inner Spirit, and a vision of Truth which gives liberation: this is true wisdom leading to vision. All against this is ignorance.

12 Now I shall tell thee of the End of wisdom. When a man knows this he goes beyond death. It is Brahman, beginningless, supreme: beyond what is and beyond what is not.

13 His hands and feet are everywhere, he has heads and mouths everywhere: he sees all, he hears all. He is in all, and he is.

14 The Light of consciousness comes to him through infinite powers of perception, and yet he is above all these powers. He is beyond all, and yet he supports all. He is beyond the world of matter, and yet he has joy in this world.

15 He is invisible: he cannot be seen. He is far and he is near, he moves and he moves not, he is within all and he is outside all.

16 He is ONE in all, but it seems as if he were many. He supports all beings: from him comes destruction, and from him comes creation.

17 He is the Light of all lights which shines beyond all darkness. It is vision, the end of vision, to be reached by vision, dwelling in the heart of all.

18 I have told thee briefly what is the field, what is wisdom,

and what is the End of man's vision. When a man knows this he enters into my Being.

19 Know that Prakriti, Nature, and Purusha, Spirit, are both without beginning, and that temporal changes and Gunas, conditions, come all from nature.

20 Nature is the source of all material things: the maker, the means of making, and the thing made. Spirit is the source of all consciousness which feels pleasure and feels pain.

21 The spirit of man when in nature feels the ever-changing conditions of nature. When he binds himself to things ever-changing, a good or evil fate whirls him round through life-in-death.

22 But the Spirit Supreme in man is beyond fate. He watches, gives blessing, bears all, feels all. He is called the Lord Supreme and the Supreme Soul.

23 He who knows in truth this Spirit and knows nature with its changing conditions, wherever this man may be he is no more whirled round by fate.

24 Some by the Yoga of meditation, and by the grace of the Spirit, see the Spirit in themselves; some by the Yoga of the vision of Truth; and others by the Yoga of work.

25 And yet there are others who do not know, but they hear from others and adore. They also cross beyond death, because of their devotion to words of Truth.

26 Whatever is born, Arjuna, whether it moves or it moves not, know that it comes from the union of the field and the knower of the field.

27 He who sees that the Lord of all is ever the same in all that is, immortal in the field of mortality – he sees the truth.

28 And when a man sees that the God in himself is the same God in all that is, he hurts not himself by hurting others: then he goes indeed to the highest Path.

29 He who sees that all work, everywhere, is only the work of nature; and that the Spirit watches this work – he sees the truth.

30 When a man sees that the infinity of various beings is abiding in the ONE, and is an evolution from the ONE, then he becomes one with Brahman.

31 Beginningless and free from changing conditions, imperishable is the Spirit Supreme. Though he is in the body, not his is the work of the body, and he is pure from the imperfection of all work.

32 Just as the omnipresent ether is pure because intangible, so the Spirit dwelling in matter is pure from the touch of matter.

33 And even as one sun gives light to all things in this world, so the Lord of the field gives light to all his field.

34 Those who with the eye of inner vision see the distinction between the field and the knower of the field, and see the liberation of spirit from matter, they go into the Supreme.

14

KRISHNA

1 I will reveal again a supreme wisdom, of all wisdom the highest: sages who have known it have gone hence to supreme perfection.

2 Taking refuge in this wisdom they have become part of me: they are not reborn at the time of creation, and they are not destroyed at the time of dissolution.

3 In the vastness of my Nature I place the seed of things to come; and from this union comes the birth of all beings.

4 Wherever a being may be born, Arjuna, know that my Nature is his mother and that I am the Father who gave him life.

5 SATTVA, RAJAS, TAMAS — light, fire, and darkness — are the three constituents of nature. They appear to limit in finite bodies the liberty of their infinite Spirit.*

6 Of these Sattva because it is pure, and it gives light and is the health of life, binds to earthly happiness and to lower knowledge.

---

* SATTVA, RAJAS, and TAMAS are the three 'Gunas', or the three 'strands' which, intertwined, are both the constituents and the changing conditions of nature. They are the light and harmony of pure intelligence and goodness; the fire and desire of impure mental energy and restless passion; and the darkness of dullness and inertia. Until final freedom is attained, they are clouds of matter darkening the Sun of the Spirit.

7 Rajas is of the nature of passion, the source of thirst and attachment. It binds the soul of man to action.

8 Tamas, which is born of ignorance, darkens the soul of all men. It binds them to sleepy dullness, and then they do not watch and then they do not work.

9 Sattva binds to happiness; Rajas to action; Tamas, over-clouding wisdom, binds to lack of vigilance.

10 Sometimes Sattva may prevail over Rajas and Tamas, at others Rajas over Tamas and Sattva, and at others Tamas over Sattva and Rajas.

11 When the light of wisdom shines from the portals of the body's dwelling, then we know that Sattva is in power.

12 Greed, busy activity, many undertakings, unrest, the lust of desire – these arise when Rajas increases.

13 Darkness, inertia, negligence, delusion – these appear when Tamas prevails.

14 If the soul meets death when Sattva prevails, then it goes to the pure regions of those who are seeking Truth.

15 If a man meets death in a state of Rajas, he is reborn amongst those who are bound by their restless activity; and if he dies in Tamas he is reborn in the wombs of the irrational.

16 Any work when it is well done bears the pure harmony of Sattva; but when done in Rajas it brings pain, and when done in Tamas it brings ignorance.

17 From Sattva arises wisdom, from Rajas greed, from Tamas negligence, delusion and ignorance.

18 Those who are in Sattva climb the path that leads on high, those who are in Rajas follow the level path, those who are in Tamas sink downwards on the lower path.

19 When the man of vision sees that the powers of nature are the only actors of this vast drama, and he beholds THAT

which is beyond the powers of nature then he comes into my Being.

20 And when he goes beyond the three conditions of nature which constitute his mortal body then, free from birth, old age, and death, and sorrow, he enters into Immortality.

ARJUNA

21 How is the man known who has gone beyond the three powers of nature? What is his path; and how does he transcend the three?

KRISHNA

22 He who hates not light, nor busy activity, nor even darkness, when they are near, neither longs for them when they are far;

23 Who unperturbed by changing conditions sits apart and watches and says 'the powers of nature go round', and remains firm and shakes not;

24 Who dwells in his inner self, and is the same in pleasure and pain; to whom gold or stones or earth are one, and what is pleasing or displeasing leave him in peace; who is beyond both praise and blame, and whose mind is steady and quiet;

25 Who is the same in honour or disgrace, and has the same love for enemies or friends, who surrenders all selfish undertakings – this man has gone beyond the three.

26 And he who with never-failing love adores me and works for me, he passes beyond the three powers and can be one with Brahman, the ONE.

27 For I am the abode of Brahman, the never-failing fountain

of everlasting life. The law of righteousness is my law; and
my joy is infinite joy.

15

1 There is a tree, the tree of Transmigration, the Asvattha tree everlasting. Its roots are above in the Highest, and its branches are here below. Its leaves are sacred songs, and he who knows them knows the Vedas.

2 Its branches spread from earth to heaven, and the powers of nature give them life. Its buds are the pleasures of the senses. Far down below, its roots stretch into the world of men, binding a mortal through selfish actions.

3 Men do not see the changing form of that tree, nor its
4 beginning, nor its end, nor where its roots are. But let the wise see, and with the strong sword of dispassion let him cut this strong-rooted tree, and seek that path wherefrom those who go never return. Such a man can say: 'I go for refuge to that Eternal Spirit from whom the stream of creation came at the beginning.'

5 Because the man of pure vision, without pride or delusion, in liberty from the chains of attachments, with his soul ever in his inner Spirit, all selfish desires gone, and free from the two contraries known as pleasure and pain, goes to the abode of Eternity.

6 There the sun shines not, nor the moon gives light, nor fire burns, for the Light of my glory is there. Those who reach that abode return no more.

7 A spark of my eternal Spirit becomes in this world a living soul; and this draws around its centre the five senses and the mind resting in nature.

8 When the Lord of the body arrives, and when he departs and wanders on, he takes them over with him, as the wind takes perfumes from their place of sleep.

9 And he watches over the mind and its senses — ear, eye, touch, and taste, and smell — and his consciousness enjoys their world.

10 When he departs, or when he stays, and with the powers of his nature enjoys life, those in delusion see him not, but he who has the eye of wisdom sees.

11 Seekers of union, ever striving, see him dwelling in their own hearts; but those who are not pure and have not wisdom, though they strive, never see him.

12 That splendour of light that comes from the sun and which illumines the whole universe, the soft light of the moon, the brightness of fire — know that they all come from me.

13 I come into the earth and with life-giving love I support all things on earth. And I become the scent and taste of the sacred plant Soma, which is the wandering moon.

14 I become the fire of life which is in all things that breathe; and in union with the breath that flows in and flows out I burn the four kinds of food.

15 And I am in the heart of all. With me come memory and wisdom, and without me they depart. I am the knower and the knowledge of the Vedas, and the creator of their end, the Vedanta.

16 There are two spirits in this universe, the perishable and the imperishable. The perishable is all things in creation. The imperishable is that which moves not.

17 But the highest spirit is another: it is called the Spirit

Supreme. He is the God of Eternity who pervading all sustains all.

18 Because I am beyond the perishable, and even beyond the imperishable, in this world and in the Vedas I am known as the Spirit Supreme.

19 He who with a clear vision sees me as the Spirit Supreme he knows all there is to be known, and he adores me with all his soul.

20 I have revealed to thee the most secret doctrine, Arjuna. He who sees it has seen light, and his task in this world is done.

16

KRISHNA

1 Freedom from fear, purity of heart, constancy in sacred learning and contemplation, generosity, self-harmony, adoration, study of the scriptures, austerity, righteousness;

2 Non-violence, truth, freedom from anger, renunciation, serenity, aversion to fault-finding, sympathy for all beings, peace from greedy cravings, gentleness, modesty, steadiness;

3 Energy, forgiveness, fortitude, purity, a good will, freedom from pride — these are the treasures of the man who is born for heaven.

4 Deceitfulness, insolence and self-conceit, anger and harshness and ignorance — these belong to a man who is born for hell.

5 The virtues of heaven are for liberation but the sins of hell are the chains of the soul. Grieve not, Arjuna, for heaven is thy final end.

6 There are two natures in this world: the one is of heaven, the other of hell. The heavenly nature has been explained: hear now of the evil of hell.

7 Evil men know not what should be done or what should not be done. Purity is not in their hearts, nor good conduct, nor truth.

8 They say: 'This world has no truth, no moral foundation,

73

no God. There is no law of creation: what is the cause of birth but lust?'

9 Firm in this belief, these men of dead souls, of truly little intelligence, undertake their work of evil: they are the enemies of this fair world, working for its destruction.

10 They torture their soul with insatiable desires and full of deceit, insolence, and pride, they hold fast their dark ideas, and they carry on their impure work.

11 Thus they are beset with innumerable cares which last long, all their life, until death. Their highest aim is sensual enjoyment, and they firmly think that this is all.

12 They are bound by hundreds of vain hopes. Anger and lust is their refuge; and they strive by unjust means to amass wealth for their own cravings.

13 'I have gained this today, and I shall attain this desire. This wealth is mine, and that shall also be mine.'

14 'I have slain that enemy, and others also shall I slay. I am a lord, I enjoy life, I am successful, powerful and happy.'

15 'I am wealthy and of noble birth: who else is there like me? I shall pay for religious rituals, I shall make benefactions, I shall enjoy myself.' Thus they say in their darkness of delusion.

16 Led astray by many wrong thoughts, entangled in the net of delusion, enchained to the pleasures of their cravings, they fall down into a foul hell.

17 In their haughtiness of vainglory, drunk with the pride of their wealth, they offer their wrong sacrifices for ostentation, against divine law.

18 In their chains of selfishness and arrogance, of violence and anger and lust, these malignant men hate me: they hate me in themselves and in others.

19 In the vast cycles of life and death I inexorably hurl them

down to destruction: these the lowest of men, cruel and evil, whose soul is hate.

20 Reborn in a lower life, in darkness birth after birth, they come not to me, Arjuna; but they go down the path of hell.

21 Three are the gates to this hell, the death of the soul: the gate of lust, the gate of wrath, and the gate of greed. Let a man shun the three.

22 When a man is free from these three doors of darkness, he does what is good for his soul, and then he enters the Path Supreme.

23 But the man who rejects the words of the Scriptures and follows the impulse of desire attains neither his perfection, nor joy, nor the Path Supreme.

24 Let the Scriptures be therefore thy authority as to what is right and what is not right. Know the words of the Scriptures, and do in this life the work to be done.

17

1 Those who forsake the law of the Scriptures and yet offer sacrifice full of faith – What is their condition, Krishna? Is it of Sattva, Rajas, or Tamas – of light, of fire, or of darkness?

KRISHNA

2 The faith of men, born of their nature, is of three kinds: of light, of fire and of darkness. Hear now of these.

3 The faith of a man follows his nature, Arjuna. Man is made of faith: as his faith is so he is.

4 Men of light worship the gods of Light; men of fire worship the gods of power and wealth; men of darkness worship ghosts and spirits of night.

5 There are men selfish and false who moved by their lusts
6 and passions perform terrible austerities not ordained by sacred books: fools who torture the powers of life in their bodies and me who dwells in them. Know that their mind is darkness.

7 Hear now of three kinds of food, the three kinds of sacrifice, the three kinds of harmony, and the three kinds of gifts.

8 Men who are pure like food which is pure: which gives

health, mental power, strength and long life; which has taste, is soothing and nourishing, and which makes glad the heart of man.

9 Men of Rajas like food of Rajas: acid and sharp, and salty and dry, and which brings heaviness and sickness and pain.

10 Men of darkness eat food which is stale and tasteless, which is rotten and left overnight, impure, unfit for holy offerings.

11 A sacrifice is pure when it is an offering of adoration in harmony with the holy law, with no expectation of a reward, and with the heart saying 'it is my duty'.

12 But a sacrifice that is done for the sake of a reward, or for the sake of vainglory is an impure sacrifice of Rajas.

13 And a sacrifice done against the holy law, without faith, and sacred words, and the gifts of food, and the due offering, is a sacrifice of darkness.

14 Reverence for the gods of Light, for the twice-born, for the teachers of the Spirit and for the wise; and also purity, righteousness, chastity and non-violence: this is the harmony of the body.

15 Words which give peace, words which are good and beautiful and true, and also the reading of sacred books: this is the harmony of words.

16 Quietness of mind, silence, self-harmony, loving-kindness, and a pure heart: this is the harmony of the mind.

17 This threefold harmony is called pure when it is practised with supreme faith with no desire for a reward and with oneness of soul.

18 But false austerity, for the sake of reputation, honour and reverence, is impure: it belongs to Rajas and is unstable and uncertain.

19 When self-control is self-torture, due to dullness of the

mind, or when it aims at hurting another, then self-control
is of darkness.

20 A gift is pure when it is given from the heart to the right
person at the right time and at the right place, and when
we expect nothing in return.

21 But when it is given expecting something in return, or for
the sake of a future reward, or when it is given unwillingly,
the gift is of Rajas, impure.

22 And a gift given to the wrong person, at the wrong time
and the wrong place, or a gift which comes not from the
heart, and is given with proud contempt, is a gift of
darkness.

23 OM, TAT, SAT. Each one of these three words is one word
for Brahman, from whom came in the beginning the
Brahmins, the Vedas and the Sacrifice.

24 Therefore with the word OM the lovers of Brahman begin
all work of sacrifice, gift or self-harmony, done according
to the Scriptures.

25 And with the word TAT, and with renunciation of all
reward, this same work of sacrifice, gift or self-harmony is
being done by those seekers of Infinite Liberty.

26 SAT is what is good and what is true: when therefore a
work is well done the end of that work is SAT.

27 Constant faithfulness in sacrifice, gift, or self-harmony is
SAT; and also all work consecrated to Brahman.

28 But work done without faith is ASAT, is nothing: sacrifice,
gift, or self-harmony done without faith are nothing, both
in this world and in the world to come.

18

1 Speak to me, Krishna, of the essence of renunciation, and of the essence of surrender.

KRISHNA

2 The renunciation of selfish works is called renunciation; but the surrender of the reward of all work is called surrender.

3 Some say that there should be renunciation of action — since action disturbs contemplation; but others say that works of sacrifice, gift and self-harmony should not be renounced.

4 Hear my truth about the surrender of works, Arjuna. Surrender, O best of men, is of three kinds.

5 Works of sacrifice, gift, and self-harmony should not be abandoned, but should indeed be performed; for these are works of purification.

6 But even these works, Arjuna, should be done in the freedom of a pure offering, and without expectation of a reward. This is my final word.

7 It is not right to leave undone the holy work which ought to be done. Such a surrender of action would be a delusion of darkness.

8 And he who abandons his duty because he has fear of pain, his surrender is of Rajas, impure, and in truth he has no reward.

9 But he who does holy work, Arjuna, because it ought to be done, and surrenders selfishness and thought of reward, his work is pure, and is peace.

10 This man sees and has no doubts: he surrenders, he is pure and has peace. Work, pleasant or painful, is for him joy.

11 For there is no man on earth who can fully renounce living work, but he who renounces the reward of his work is in truth a man of renunciation.

12 When work is done for a reward, the work brings pleasure, or pain, or both, in its time; but when a man does work in Eternity, then Eternity is his reward.

13 Know now from me, Arjuna, the five causes of all actions as given in the Sankhya wisdom, wherein is found the end of all works.

14 The body, the lower 'I am', the means of perception, the means of action, and Fate. These are the five.

15 Whatever a man does, good or bad, in thought, word or deed, has these five sources of action.

16 If one thinks that his infinite Spirit does the finite work which nature does, he is a man of clouded vision and he does not see the truth.

17 He who is free from the chains of selfishness, and whose mind is free from any ill-will, even if he kills all these warriors he kills them not and he is free.

18 In the idea of a work there is the knower, the knowing and the known. When the idea is work there is the doer, the doing and the thing done.

19 The knowing, the doer and the thing done are said in the

science of the 'Gunas' to be of three kinds, according to their qualities. Hear of these three.

20 When one sees Eternity in things that pass away and Infinity in finite things, then one has pure knowledge.

21 But if one merely sees the diversity of things, with their divisions and limitations, then one has impure knowledge.

22 And if one selfishly sees a thing as if it were everything, independent of the ONE and the many, then one is in the darkness of ignorance.

23 When work is done as sacred work, unselfishly, with a peaceful mind, without lust or hate, with no desire for reward, then the work is pure.

24 But when work is done with selfish desire, or feeling it is an effort, or thinking it is a sacrifice, then the work is impure.

25 And that work which is done with a confused mind, without considering what may follow, or one's own powers, or the harm done to others, or one's own loss, is work of darkness.

26 A man free from the chains of selfish attachments, free from his lower 'I am', who has determination and perseverance, and whose inner peace is beyond victory or defeat – such a man has pure Sattva.

27 But a man who is a slave of his passions, who works for selfish ends, who is greedy, violent and impure, and who is moved by pleasure and pain, is a man of impure Rajas.

28 And a man without self-harmony, vulgar, arrogant and deceitful; malicious, indolent and despondent, and also procrastinating, is a man of the darkness of Tamas.

29 Hear now fully and in detail the threefold division of wisdom and steadiness, according to the three Gunas.

30 There is a wisdom which knows when to go and when to

return, what is to be done and what is not to be done, what is fear and what is courage, what is bondage and what is liberation – that is pure wisdom.

31 Impure wisdom has no clear vision of what is right and what is wrong, what should be done and what should not be done.

32 And there is a wisdom obscured in darkness when wrong is thought to be right, and when things are thought to be that which they are not.

33 When in the Yoga of holy contemplation the movements of the mind and of the breath of life are in a harmony of peace, there is steadiness, and that steadiness is pure.

34 But that steadiness which, with a desire for rewards, attaches itself to wealth, pleasure, and even religious ritual, is a steadiness of passion, impure.

35 And that steadiness whereby a fool does not surrender laziness, fear, self-pity, depression and lust, is indeed a steadiness of darkness.

36 Hear now, great Arjuna, of the three kinds of pleasure. There is the pleasure of following that right path which leads to the end of all pain.

37 What seems at first a cup of sorrow is found in the end immortal wine. That pleasure is pure: it is the joy which arises from a clear vision of the Spirit.

38 But the pleasure which comes from the craving of the senses with the objects of their desire, which seems at first a drink of sweetness but is found in the end a cup of poison, is the pleasure of passion, impure.

39 And that pleasure which both in the beginning and in the end is only a delusion of the soul, which comes from the dullness of sleep, laziness or carelessness, is the pleasure of darkness.

40 There is nothing on earth or in heaven which is free from these three powers of Nature.

41 The works of Brahmins, Kshatriyas, Vaisyas and Sudras are different, in harmony with the three powers of their born nature.

42 The works of a Brahmin are peace; self-harmony, austerity and purity; loving-forgiveness and righteousness; vision and wisdom and faith.

43 These are the works of a Kshatriya: a heroic mind, inner fire, constancy, resourcefulness, courage in battle, generosity and noble leadership.

44 Trade, agriculture and the rearing of cattle is the work of a Vaisya. And the work of the Sudra is service.

45 They all attain perfection when they find joy in their work. Hear how a man attains perfection and finds joy in his work.

46 A man attains perfection when his work is worship of God, from whom all things come and who is in all.

47 Greater is thine own work, even if this be humble, than the work of another, even if this be great. When a man does the work God gives him, no sin can touch this man.

48 And a man should not abandon his work, even if he cannot achieve it in full perfection; because in all work there may be imperfection, even as in all fire there is smoke.

49 When a man has his reason in freedom from bondage, and his soul is in harmony, beyond desires, then renunciation leads him to a region supreme which is beyond earthly action.

50 Hear now how he then reaches Brahman, the highest vision of Light.

51 When the vision of reason is clear, and in steadiness the soul is in harmony; when the world of sound and other

senses is gone, and the spirit has risen above passion and hate;

52 When a man dwells in the solitude of silence, and meditation and contemplation are ever with him; when too much food does not disturb his health, and his thoughts and words and body are in peace; when freedom from passion is his constant will;

53 And his selfishness and violence and pride are gone; when lust and anger and greediness are no more, and he is free from the thought 'this is mine'; then this man has risen on the mountain of the Highest: he is worthy to be one with Brahman, with God.

54 He is one with Brahman, with God, and beyond grief and desire his soul is in peace. His love is one for all creation, and he has supreme love for me.

55 By love he knows me in truth, who I am and what I am. And when he knows me in truth he enters into my Being.

56 In whatever work he does he can take refuge in me, and he attains then by my grace the imperishable home of Eternity.

57 Offer in thy heart all thy works to me, and see me as the End of thy love, take refuge in the Yoga of reason, and ever rest thy soul in me.

58 If thy soul finds rest in me, thou shalt overcome all dangers by my grace; but if thy thoughts are on thyself, and thou wilt not listen, thou shalt perish.

59 If thou wilt not fight thy battle of life because in selfishness thou art afraid of the battle, thy resolution is in vain: nature will compel thee.

60 Because thou art in the bondage of Karma, of the forces of thine own past life; and that which thou, in thy delusion, with a good will dost not want to do, unwillingly thou shalt have to do.

61 God dwells in the heart of all beings, Arjuna: thy God dwells in thy heart. And his power of wonder moves all things – puppets in a play of shadows – whirling them onwards on the stream of time.

62 Go to him for thy salvation with all thy soul, victorious man. By his grace thou shalt obtain the peace supreme, thy home of Eternity.

63 I have given thee words of vision and wisdom more secret than hidden mysteries. Ponder them in the silence of thy soul, and then in freedom do thy will.

64 Hear again my Word supreme, the deepest secret of silence. Because I love thee well, I will speak to thee words of salvation.

65 Give thy mind to me, and give me thy heart, and thy sacrifice, and thy adoration. This is my Word of promise: thou shalt in truth come to me, for thou art dear to me.

66 Leave all things behind, and come to me for thy salvation. I will make thee free from the bondage of sins. Fear no more.

67 These things must never be spoken to one who lacks self-discipline, or who has no love, or who does not want to hear or who argues against me.

68 But he who will teach this secret doctrine to those who have love for me, and who himself has supreme love, he in truth shall come unto me.

69 For there can be no man among men who does greater work for me, nor can there be a man on earth who is dearer to me than he is.

70 He who learns in contemplation the holy words of our discourse, the light of his vision is his adoration. This is my truth.

71 And he who only hears but has faith, and in his heart he

has no doubts, he also attains liberation and the worlds of joy of righteous men.

72 Hast thou heard these words, Arjuna, in the silent communion of thy soul? Has the darkness of thy delusion been dispelled by thine inner Light?

ARJUNA

73 By thy grace I remember my Light, and now gone is my delusion. My doubts are no more, my faith is firm; and now I can say 'Thy will be done.'

SANJAYA

74 Thus I heard these words of glory between Arjuna and the God of all, and they fill my soul with awe and wonder.

75 By the grace of the poet Vyasa I heard these words of secret silence. I heard the mystery of Yoga, taught by Krishna the Master himself.

76 I remember, O king, I remember the words of holy wonder between Krishna and Arjuna, and again and again my soul feels joy.

77 And I remember, I ever remember, that vision of glory of the God of all, and again and again joy fills my soul.

78 Wherever is Krishna, the End of Yoga, wherever is Arjuna who masters the bow, there is beauty and victory, and joy and all righteousness. This is my faith.

READ MORE IN PENGUIN

HOMER
The Iliad

One of the foremost achievements in Western literature, Homer's *Iliad* tells the story of the darkest episode in the Trojan War. At its centre is Achilles, the greatest warrior-champion of the Greeks, and his refusal to fight after being humiliated by his leader Agamemnon. But when the Trojan Hector kills Achilles' close friend Patroclus, he storms back into battle to take revenge – although knowing this will ensure his own early death. Interwoven with this tragic sequence of events are powerfully moving descriptions of the ebb and flow of battle, of the domestic world inside Troy's besieged city of Ilium and of the conflicts between the gods on Olympus as they argue over the fate of mortals.

E. V. Rieu's acclaimed translation of Homer's *The Iliad* was one of the first titles published in Penguin Classics, and now has classic status itself. For this edition, Rieu's text has been revised, and a new introduction and notes by Peter Jones complement the original introduction.

Translated by E. V. RIEU
Revised and updated by PETER JONES *with* D. C. H. RIEU
Edited with an introduction and notes by PETER JONES

HOMER

The Odyssey

The epic tale of Odysseus and his ten-year journey home after the Trojan War forms one of the earliest and greatest works of Western literature. Confronted by natural and supernatural threats – shipwrecks, battles, monsters and the implacable enmity of the sea-god Poseidon – Odysseus must test his bravery and native cunning to the full if he is to reach his homeland safely and overcome the obstacles that, even there, await him.

E. V. Rieu's translation of *The Odyssey* was the very first Penguin Classic to be published, and has itself achieved classic status. For this edition, Rieu's text has been sensitively revised and a new introduction added to complement his original introduction.

'One of the world's most vital tales ... The Odyssey remains central to literature' MALCOLM BRADBURY

Translated by E. V. RIEU
Revised translation by D. C. H. RIEU
With an introduction by PETER JONES

Beowulf
A Verse Translation

Beowulf is the greatest surviving work of literature in Old English, unparalleled in its epic grandeur and scope. It tells the story of the heroic Beowulf and of his battles, first with the monster Grendel, who has laid waste to the great hall of the Danish king Hrothgar, then with Grendel's avenging mother, and finally with a dragon that threatens to devastate his homeland. Through its blend of myth and history, *Beowulf* vividly evokes a twilight world in which men and supernatural forces live side by side, and celebrates the endurance of the human spirit in a transient world.

Michael Alexander's landmark modern English verse translation has been revised to take account of new readings and interpretations. His new introduction discusses central themes of *Beowulf* and its place among epic poems, the history of its publication and reception, and issues of translation.

'A foundation stone of poetry in English' ANDREW MOTION

Revised edition

Translated with an introduction and notes by
MICHAEL ALEXANDER

TRANSLATED BY JOHN DRYDEN

Virgil's Aeneid

Dryden's *Æneis* (1697), writes Frederick Keener, is not merely a superb translation but 'an important, magisterial and moving English poem' in its own right, as well as a major influence on Pope and the main eighteenth-century tradition.

In Aeneas, Virgil created the most powerful figure in Latin literature, the dutiful yet fallible Trojan prince who overcomes war, suffering and countless setbacks to lay the foundations of the Roman race. Like many of his generation, John Dryden (1631–1700) believed the great classical epics could provide moral models to 'form the Mind to Heroick Virtue by Example'. For his version of the *Aeneid*, he formed a style vigorous yet refined and drew on the deep understanding of political unrest he had acquired during the Civil Wars of 1642–51 and the Glorious Revolution of 1688. This Penguin English Poets edition includes maps, a substantial glossary and enough background to help readers overcome any unfamiliarity with style or substance, thus making freshly accessible a work of enduring worth.

Edited by FREDERICK M. KEENER